Marxist Introductions

General Editors
Raymond Williams
Steven Lukes

Also published in this series

Marxism and Literature   by Raymond Williams
Marxism and Politics   by Ralph Miliband
Marxism and Law   by Hugh Collins
Marxism and Anthropology   by Maurice Bloch

Marxism and Philosophy

Alex Callinicos

Clarendon Press · Oxford
1983

Oxford University Press, Walton Street, Oxford OX2 6DP

London Glasgow New York Toronto
Delhi Bombay Calcutta Madras Karachi
Kuala Lumpur Singapore Hong Kong Tokyo
Nairobi Dar es Salaam Cape Town
Melbourne Auckland

and associates in
Beirut Berlin Ibadan Mexico City Nicosia

Oxford is a trade mark of Oxford University Press

Published in the United States by
Oxford University Press, New York

British Library Cataloguing in Publication Data

Callinicos, Alex
  Marxism and philosophy. — (Marxist introductions)
  1. Communism
  I. Title   II. Series
  335.4'01   HX73
  ISBN 0-19-876126-0

Library of Congress Cataloging in Publication Data
Callinicos, Alex.
  Marxism and philosophy.
  (Marxist introductions)
  Includes bibliographical references and index.
  1. Communism and philosophy. 2. Marx, Karl,
1818-1883. I. Title. II. Series.
HX533.C34 1983   335.43'01   82-18767
ISBN 0-19-876126-0

Typeset by Cotswold Typesetting Ltd., Cheltenham,
Printed in Great Britain by
Billings and Sons Ltd.
London and Worcester.

Preface

This book attempts an overview of Marxist philosophy. In doing so, it pursues a series of reflections on the philosophical problems posed by Marxism which began in my first book, *Althusser's Marxism*, and was continued in my doctoral thesis, 'The Logic of Capital', and another book, *Is There a Future for Marxism?* Any novelty it may possess lies in the exploration in the second half of the book of some of the connections between these problems and recent developments in analytical philosophy. In a book of this length, I have often been compelled only to sketch out arguments, rather than develop them in any detail, but the result may still be of some interest.

I am grateful to Steven Lukes and Raymond Williams, the editors of this series; to Colin Sparks, who encouraged me to start out on the project in the first place; to the Master and Fellows of St. Peter's College, Oxford, where, as a Junior Research Fellow, I wrote this book; and, especially, to Mike Rosen, with whom my many conversations greatly clarified thoughts on the subject-matter of this book, and to Joanna Seddon, who put up with me while I wrote it, and suggested many improvements in the manuscript.

Two more general debts should be acknowledged: to Alan Montefiore, who initiated me, along with so many others, into the mysteries of continental philosophy, and to Tony Cliff, Duncan Hallas, Chris Harman, Nigel Harris, and Mike Kidron, to whom I owe much of my understanding of Marxism. It should go without saying that none of the aforementioned are responsible for this consequence of their help and encouragement.

One final name cannot go unmentioned, even though I am unacquainted with its bearer. It is to Louis Althusser more than to any other individual or group that we owe the current renaissance of Marxist philosophy. It is, therefore, to him, despite my many disagreements with him over theoretical and political issues, and in the face of the tragedy that has now engulfed him, that I wish to dedicate this book.

Alex Callinicos

Contents

KEY TO ABBREVIATIONS

C   Marx, *Capital* (3 vols.: i Harmondsworth, 1976, ii Moscow 1956, iii Moscow, 1971)

CPR Kant, *Critique of Pure Reason* (London, 1970)

CW   Marx and Engels, *Collected Works* (50 vols. published or in preparation, London, 1975-)

FM   L. Althusser, *For Marx* (London, 1969)

G   Marx, *Grundrisse* (Harmondsworth, 1973)

GL   G. W. F. Hegel, *The Science of Logic* (2 vols., London, 1929)

HCC G. Lukács, *History and Class Consciousness* (London, 1971)

LL   *The Logic of Hegel* (Oxford, 1975)

ND   T. W. Adorno, *Negative Dialectics* (London, 1973)

RC   L. Althusser and E. Balibar, *Reading Capital* (London, 1970)

SC   Marx and Engels, *Selected Correspondence* (Moscow, 1975)

SW   Marx and Engels, *Selected Works* (3 vols., Moscow, 1973)

TSV Marx, *Theories of Surplus-Value* (3 vols., Moscow, 1963–72)

Introduction

A book devoted to Marxism and philosophy suffers from peculiar difficulties. For although Marx began his intellectual career as a philosopher, and in his early writings confronted the philosophical views of his immediate predecessors and contemporaries, the texts in which historical materialism first took shape brusquely turned their back, not merely on one or another philosophical school, but on philosophy itself. Everyone knows the eleventh thesis on Feuerbach: 'The philosophers have only *interpreted* the world in various ways; the point is to *change* it.' (*CW* 5:5.) Marx and Engels were even less complimentary in *The German Ideology*: 'Philosophy and the study of the actual world have the same relation to one another as onanism and sexual love.' (Ibid. 236.) These statements announced what the authors believed to be their final and irrevocable departure from speculation's realm of shades for the firm ground of empirical science, whose premises are not the abstractions of philosophy, but 'the real individuals, their activity and the material conditions of their life', and 'can thus be verified in a purely empirical way' (ibid. 31).

It is one of the many paradoxes of Marxism's history that this parting of the ways between philosophy and historical materialism seems never to have been finally accomplished. Indeed, what is striking is how often Marxist thinkers have responded to the theoretical and political difficulties by appealing to philosophical categories and doctrines. This tendency is often said to be peculiar to 'Western' Marxists, a predominantly academic, and unquestionably a philosophically inclined group of thinkers which emerged on the Continent between the 1920s and 1960s.[1] The temptation for Marxist theoreticians to retreat into philosophy seems, however, more deep-rooted than this interpretation would suggest.

To take the most striking example, in August 1914 Lenin's world fell apart. The outbreak of the First World War saw the parties of the second International defy resolutions reaffirmed at

1

congress after congress and support their respective national governments rather than unite against the slaughter. Even the German Social Democratic party (SPD), the citadel of international Marxism, voted for the Imperial Government's war-credits in the Reichstag. This crisis helped to push Lenin away from the evolutionist version of Marxism embodied by Karl Kautsky, intellectual pope of the SPD and the second International. Lenin's reorientation took a strange form for so practical a revolutionary. As the cannon thundered across Europe, and the international working-class movement disintegrated, he retreated to the public library at Berne to study Hegel. The result was the *Philosophical Notebooks,* published posthumously, where Lenin announced: '*Aphorism*: It is impossible completely to understand Marx's *Capital,* and especially its first chapter, without having understood the *whole* of Hegel's *Logic.* Consequently, half a century later [i.e., after the publication of *Capital* Volume i in 1867] none of the Marxists understood Marx!'[2]

This claim, that Hegel's dialectic is indispensable to the understanding of the work of Marx's maturity, finds confirmation in a letter from Marx to Engels of January 1858, at a time when the financial crash of the previous year, which the two friends hoped was the prelude to an upsurge of revolution, had led Marx to resume his economic studies: 'The fact that by mere accident I again glanced through Hegel's *Logic* (Freilgrath found some volumes of Hegel which originally belonged to Bakunin and sent them to me as a present) has been of great service to me as regards the *method* of dealing with the material.' (*SC* 93.) And indeed the manuscript which emerged from these studies, the *Grundrisse* or rough draft of *Capital,* first published in 1939–40, is the most Hegelian of all Marx's writings. He sought to defend the presence of Hegelian categories in *Capital* Volume 1 itself by distinguishing between the 'rational kernel' and 'mystical shell' of Hegel's dialectic (*C* i.103). In the letter to Engels cited above, Marx expressed a wish to go beyond such metaphors: 'If there should ever be time for such work again, I should very much like to make accessible to the ordinary human intelligence – in two or three printer's sheets – what is *rational* in the method which Hegel developed but at the same time enveloped in mysticism.' (*SC* 93.)

There never was time, but here we stand at the threshold of Marxist philosophy, a discipline whose very existence might seem questionable from the standpoint of Marx's and Engels's repudiation of all philosophy in the mid-1840s, but which has constituted itself around the questions posed by Marx's failure to clarify his relation to Hegel. The most important and influential Marxist philosophical works – Engels's *Anti-Dühring*, Lukács's *History and Class Consciousness*, Althusser's *For Marx* and *Reading Capital*, Adorno's *Negative Dialectics* – have all been concerned with precisely these questions. Marx wrote that Hegel was 'the last word of all philosophy',[3] and indeed Hegel has played the role of *the* philosopher for Marxists, which Aristotle did for the medieval schoolmen. Vulgarized versions of Hegel's *Logic* provide much of the content of Soviet textbooks of 'dialectical materialism', while accusations of a failure to understand 'the dialectic' have been the common currency of Marxist polemic from Plekhanov's day to our own.

Situating Marxist philosophy in terms of Marx's relation to Hegel introduces an additional difficulty for any discussion of the subject written in English. Analytical philosophy, the cluster of schools predominant among English-speaking philosophers, took as one of its starting-points the critique of Hegelianism, in the form of the logical and metaphysical doctrines of F. H. Bradley and other British idealists, by Bertrand Russell and G. E. Moore at the turn of the nineteenth century. Most, if not all, analytical philosophers would agree with the Wykeham Professor of Logic at Oxford, Michael Dummett: 'it is undoubtedly true that the overthrow of Hegelianism was a precondition of advance in philosophy'.[4] Here, then, is a fundamental divide between Marxist and analytical philosophers, for the former, even if anti-Hegelian, remain largely part of a tradition stemming from German classical idealism (Kant, Fichte, Schelling, Hegel) and its heirs. In certain very important respects, however, analytical philosophy is at odds with this tradition, as I shall try to show in Chapter 1.

Not surprisingly, contact between Marxist and analytical philosophers, on the rare occasions that it has occurred, has been a veritable dialogue of the deaf. Theodor Adorno found himself in Oxford in 1934–8 as a refugee from Nazi Germany. He wrote to a friend in October 1934:

> Merton College here, the oldest and most exclusive at Oxford, has taken me in as a member and 'advanced student' and I live here now in indescribable peace and under very pleasant working conditions;

with regard to the material, there are of course difficulties, as making actual philosophical things comprehensible to the English counts among the impossibilities, and to a certain extent I have to screw back my work to a child's level in order to remain intelligible.[5]

A quarter of a century later, Adorno and other members of the Frankfurt school became involved in a bitter debate with Karl Popper and his followers over the method of the social sciences – the so-called *Positivismusstreit*. Here mutual incomprehension seems to have been complete.[6]

The apparent impossibility of communication between the Marxist and analytical traditions would matter less if academic philosophy in the English-speaking world were as poverty stricken as its critics have often depicted it. Perry Anderson, in an influential essay first published in 1968, excoriated the 'parish-pump positivism' of the Vienna Circle, and the 'technicism', 'philistinism', and 'chloroforming ideology' of Oxford ordinary-language philosophy, which he depicted as the prisoner of bourgeois common sense, unable to envisage any change in the linguistic practices it so scrupulously investigated.[7] The alternative, Anderson suggested, was to embrace Western Marxism; and, indeed, the growth of interest in Marxist philosophy in the English-speaking world since the late 1960s has largely taken the form of adherence to one or another of the schools of continental Marxism. The greatest influence on British Marxists has been the work of Louis Althusser, while the Frankfurt school appears to have had more impact in the United States.

Meanwhile analytical philosophy has steamed ahead, if anything more confident of the validity of its methods. The note struck by P. F. Strawson in his 1969 inaugural lecture as Waynflete Professor of Metaphysical Philosophy at Oxford was not one of self-doubt or despair: 'During the last quarter of a century Oxford has occupied, or reoccupied, a position it last held, perhaps, six hundred years ago: that of a great centre of philosophy in the western world.'[8] Even if Anderson's strictures against analytical philosophy were just at the time of writing (and his treatment of two major figures, Wittgenstein and Popper, was grossly unfair) they no longer apply today. The past fifteen years have seen developments of the most fundamental importance in English-speaking (and especially American) philosophy – the attempt to construct a systematic theory of meaning (Davidson, Dummett), the causal theory of names (Kripke, Putnam, Donnellan), and the associated revival of epistemological realism, the emergence of anti-empiricist philosophies of science (Lakatos, Feyerabend, Kuhn), the reconstruction of bourgeois political and legal philosophy (Rawls, Nozick, Dworkin, Raz), the debates provoked by Quine's critique of meaning and Chomsky's transformational grammar. None of these developments can be dismissed as trivial or pedantic. Collectively, they have drawn analytical philosophy away from the worst excesses of logical positivism and the ordinary-language approach – respectively, vulgar empiricism and complacent lexicography – towards epistemological and metaphysical issues of substance.

Yet all this has passed English-speaking Marxist philosophers by. A growing number, trained in analytical techniques, have sought to employ them in resolving conceptual difficulties within Marxism.[9] The majority have preferred to operate within one of the continental traditions, adding footnotes to Lukács, or Adorno, or Althusser. Even when they have criticized their masters, it has been from the standpoint of some other continental thinker: thus, disillusioned Althusserians have gravitated towards Michel Foucault. Rarely, if at all, has any English-speaking Marxist been prepared to confront the analytical tradition head on (a possible exception is the philosophy of science, in any case one of the least naturalized branches of academic philosophy).[10] This is all the more strange in the light of the increasing interest shown in the philosophy of language by many academic Marxists in the Anglo-Saxon world, albeit in the form developed by the French 'post-structuralists', notably Jacques Derrida. The self-confidence and parochialism of the analytical philosophers have been mirrored by the fascination of English-speaking Marxist philosophers with continental *exotica*, leaving the mainstream of Anglo-Saxon philosophy little affected by the revival of Marxism since 1968. This is in marked contrast with what has happened in other disciplines – history, where Marxism has been well entrenched for a generation; economics, where, partly thanks to Sraffa and his school, it is now regarded as at least a respectable point of view; sociology, which seems at times almost to have been taken by storm by varieties of Western Marxism; and cultural studies, which the latter helped to invent. Marxist philosophy, however, has been confined to a ghetto, of methodological interest to

Marxists in other subjects (indeed, the entire renaissance of Marxism in the past decade and a half has been characteristically 'Western Marxist' in its philosophical bent), but incapable of making any impact on the debates among analytical philosophers. The journal of dissident British academic philosophers, *Radical Philosophy*, after including a few largely anecdotal and sociological criticisms of the mainstream tradition in its early numbers, has subsequently gone its own way, acting, as Edward Thompson put it in a related context, as an import–export agency for continental ideas, content to rely on the assertion in its first issue that 'contemporary British philosophy is at a dead end'.

The greatest irony of all is the growing interest in analytical philosophy expressed by the continental thinkers to whom English-speaking Marxists have looked for salvation. Thus in France the crisis of Althusserian Marxism, disillusionment with post-structuralism, and disgust at the antics of the *nouveaux philosophes* have led to a revulsion against what Jacques Bouveresse has called 'the megalomania, assumption of prophetic powers, and dramatization [which] have for a long time already been essential characteristics of philosophical style'.[11] The distinctive virtues of analytical philosophy – clarity, modesty, a concern for logical rigour – have suddenly seemed more attractive after the apocalyptic obscurities of Lacan and Derrida. The 1970s saw the publication of French translations of Wittgenstein, Popper, Quine, and others. *Critique*, a journal which has in the past carried major articles by or on Derrida, Deleuze and Foucault, has published a special issue devoted to *Les philosophes anglo-saxons par eux-mêmes* and a number of articles such as the one entitled 'Davidson en perspective'.[12] In Germany, one wing of the Frankfurt school, once the most bitter opponent of Anglo-Saxon 'positivism', has now drawn closer to analytical philosophy than would have been imaginable a few years ago. One is more likely to find the names of J. L. Austin and John Searle in the recent writings of Jürgen Habermas than those of Lukács and Adorno. The interest has been reciprocated by some on the dissident wing of analytical philosophy, such as Richard Rorty and Ian Hacking.

I am not suggesting that Marxist philosophers in the English-speaking world embrace Frege and Wittgenstein as uncritically as they once did Althusser and the Frankfurt school. Many of the charges made by Anderson and others against mainstream Anglo-

Saxon philosophy can be justified. But unless one thinks that Hegel was indeed the 'last philosopher' and that everything written since his time by academic philosophers is reactionary rubbish[13] (and I do not believe this, for reasons that may become apparent in the course of this book), it is incumbent upon Marxists who are interested in the development of historical materialism, rather than the incantation of received formulae, to confront critically, and seek to appropriate the positive elements of, the most advanced forms of bourgeois thought. Obviously, this is a complex, difficult, and risky process, but it must be attempted: Marxism has developed from such confrontations with bourgeois thought as well as from empirical enquiry and contact with the class struggle. I cannot claim to have made the attempt in this book, but I hope that I have indicated some of the main points of contact, and of divergence, between the Marxist and the analytical traditions. With this view, Chapter 1 outlines, in very broad strokes, some of the principal features of the Hegelian and post-Fregean traditions from which Marxist and analytical philosophy respectively sprang.

In Chapter 2 our concern with Marxism proper begins: here I consider Marx's peculiar trajectory – out of philosophy and into the new science of historical materialism, and the politics of proletarian revolution, in the 1840s, and then back to Hegel in the economic writings leading up to *Capital*. Some substantive issues – for example, the status of Marx's theory of human nature – will emerge in the course of this chapter. There follows, in Chapter 3, a review of the subsequent returns to philosophy by later Marxists. I have been forced to select ruthlessly here, and therefore have concentrated – after a survey of the 'orthodox' Marxism of the second International and its revolutionary, revisionist and Austro-Marxist progeny – on the three most substantial Marxist philosophers of the twentieth century: Georg Lukács, Theodor Adorno, and Louis Althusser.

The last three chapters move from a historical to a thematic treatment of the subject, dealing in particular with those issues where there are points of contact between problems in Marxism and discussions among analytical philosophers. Chapters 4 and 5 seek to clarify the sense in which Marxism is a materialism, dealing respectively with the different elements of the doctrines of naturalism and realism. Finally, Chapter 6 critically examines French and Anglo-Saxon philosophies of language, and considers their bearing on Marxist theories of ideology. A brief conclusion discusses the status of Marxist philosophy itself.

This last question is one that has been much on my mind in writing this book. For there is no doubt that this is what the Marx of *The German Ideology* would have called a philosophical book in the pejorative sense, concerned with the content of doctrines, the structure of arguments, and not their material conditions. Even if one recalls that Marx would have been the first to reject a vulgar reductionism that denied theoretical discourse any truth-value independent of the social relations in which it is produced, there remains the difficulty that a series such as this, and especially the volume devoted to Marxism and philosophy, is peculiarly vulnerable to appropriation by, and incorporation into, the bourgeois academy, to the transformation of Marxism into a subject of doctoral theses, into one 'approach' to a variety of intellectual problems. The problem is especially acute for someone such as myself, perhaps more committed than other contributors to this series to the classical Marxism of Marx and Engels, Lenin and Trotsky, Luxemburg, and Gramsci, both as a theoretical tradition, and as a strategy for the revolutionary overthrow of capitalist power by the working class. I have sought, therefore, to stress in Chapter 2 how Marx's philosophical development arose as much from his experience of political and social struggles as it did from any intellectual evolution. Historical materialism as it emerged from this process was conceived by its founders as the *scientific theory of working-class self-emancipation*. Its subsequent history has been a constant battle to preserve and develop both the poles of Marxism: its scientific status, and its *raison d'être* in the life and struggle of the working class. It is in this light that the Marxist philosophers discussed in this book must be evaluated; it is from this viewpoint also that the book itself must be judged.

1. Two Traditions

(1) From Kant to Hegel

'What is philosophy? Even for a professional philosopher this question is very difficult to answer,' writes A. J. Ayer.[1] Yet I think that such a philosopher would, if pressed, reply along the following lines. Scientists working in specific disciplines such as biology or physics seek to establish what kinds of object are to be found in the universe, and to uncover the internal structures of these kinds; philosophers are concerned with what it is to be an object at all. Scientists investigate particular causal connections; philosophers ask what it is to be a cause. Scientists pursue knowledge; philosophers consider what knowledge is, and whether it is possible. In W. V. O. Quine's words, 'philosophy seeks the broad outlines of the whole system of the world.'[2]

Such an account of philosophy rests on the presumption that one can distinguish between the form and the content of knowledge. What is involved in this contrast between form and content may be illustrated by a metaphor. Philosophy provides the framework of knowledge; the sciences fill in the details. As it stands, the metaphor is ambiguous: is this framework to be seen as a scaffolding, which is removed once the building is completed, or as the steel skeleton around which many modern buildings are constructed? In fact, (to continue the metaphor) the claim that philosophy establishes the form of knowledge is very often taken as meaning that in doing so she provides the sciences with a secure foundation. The distinction between form and content is also closely connected with a difference in the manner in which philosophy and the sciences proceed. Scientific knowledge is *a posteriori*, resulting from the refutation or corroboration of hypotheses by empirical evidence. Philosophy, on the other hand, is an *a priori* discipline whose propositions are arrived at by derivation from self-evident first principles or the analysis of concepts, rather than by means of observation and empirical enquiry.

There is an element of caricature in this picture of philosophy. Nevertheless, I believe it captures some of the most important aspects of the conception of philosophy accepted in the Western World in the last two centuries. This conception is a historically specific one: the discontinuity it posits between philosophy and the sciences is, for example, comparatively new. Thus in Aristotle there is no sharp break between physics and metaphysics, both are part of the same enquiry. The knowledge of particulars consists in the discovery of their final causes, or purposes, which reveals their place in the total order of the universe: there is, therefore, no fundamental difference between the exploration of details and the discovery of the fundamental structure of being in Aristotle. Philosophy proper only gradually disengaged itself from natural philosophy. Often we read the distinction in retrospect into works which do not themselves make it, so that one very widely used English translation of Descartes's *Principles of Philosophy* omits those passages which the editors regard as being concerned with physics and therefore not of philosophical interest.[3]

It is, however, with Descartes that the conception of philosophy outlined above originated. The *cogito* involved a transformation in the Western concept of the mental.[4] Previously the mind had been identified with the intellect, conceived as being inseparable from its exercise in the study of the external world; sense-perceptions, pains, dreams, etc. were not regarded by Aristotle and the medieval schoolmen as mental phenomena, but considered to be attributes of the human body. Descartes overturned this tradition, expanding the concept of the mental to include sense-impressions as well as reasoning, and asserting we are directly acquainted only with the contents of our consciousness; knowledge of the physical world is parasitic upon that of our inner states. The human mind was cut loose from the body, and transformed into a private self certain only of its own thoughts and sensations.

This move inevitably posed the problem of how our knowledge of the external world is possible, if we only have access to our private mental states. How to escape from the closed circle of inner subjectivity to the public world of objects? It was thus that modern Western philosophy took shape around the question of the foundations of knowledge. The classical British empiricists – Locke, Berkeley, and Hume – shared Descartes's starting point. Like him, they regarded the individual subject as having privileged access to the contents of its consciousness, and therefore believed that what is given in inner experience provides the only secure basis on which knowledge can rest. However, Locke and Hume in particular also believed that the task of grounding human knowledge was an essentially empirical enquiry involving an application to the study of mind of the inductive method which they thought Newton had used with such success in the realm of natural philosophy. They did not, in other words, make the distinction, which I have suggested is involved in the notion of philosophy founding the sciences, between a priori and a posteriori knowledge. Philosophy was, especially for Hume, continuous with the sciences, using the same empirical methods. A causal account of the workings of the human mind would serve to ground the sciences. Kant wrote with perfect justice of 'a certain physiology of the human understanding – that of the celebrated Locke' (CPR Aix). Hume was quite explicit in this respect. His Treatise of Human Nature is subtitled 'An Attempt to Introduce the Experimental Method of Reasoning to Moral Subjects', in other words, to provide the sciences with a secure foundation by means of an empirical, inductive account of man.[5]

It is with Hume, however, that the paradoxical nature of an attempt to ground knowledge simply by extending its domain to embrace the workings of the human mind became clear. Locke had admitted two sources of knowledge, experience and reflection; Hume's radical empiricism took him further, leading him to deny reflection any status independent of experience, and to treat ideas, the concepts with which we reason, as the faded copies of our immediate sense-impressions. Further, he argued that there is nothing in our direct experience corresponding to concepts as essential to the common-sense and scientific view of the world as that of the necessary connection between cause and effect, and of material and mental substances. We cannot rationally justify our belief in the existence of the causally governed, objective world revealed by Newtonian physics: this belief is a product of habit, of the association of ideas induced in us by the constant conjunction of certain sense-impressions. But the very concept of association of ideas essential to Hume's psychological account of the formation of habit is itself modelled on that of Newtonian gravitation,[6] and seems to involve the same concept of causality to which Hume had denied any rational justification. The science of man, which is to found the rest of knowledge, turns out to be itself without foundation.

Kant's resolution of this crisis involved distinguishing sharply between pure and empirical knowledge, and therefore between philosophy and the sciences. Like the empiricists, he followed Descartes in taking the human subject as basic. Philosophy is concerned with the conditions of possible *experience*, not with possibility and necessity *tout court* (as in Leibniz). Its task, however, is 'to institute a tribunal which will assure to reason its lawful claims', which in examining our :concepts is concerned with 'the question of right (*quid juris*)' and not 'the question of fact (*quid facti*)' (*CPR* Axi, A84/B116). The latter is Locke's and Hume's question; their answer 'shows the manner in which a concept is acquired   through   experience   and   through   reflection   on experience, and which therefore concerns, not its legitimacy, but only its *de facto* mode of origination' (ibid. A85/B117). Philosophy proper,   unlike   empirical   psychology,   is   concerned   with   a concept's *right* to exist: it must explain 'how *subjective conditions of thought* can have *objective validity*, that is, can furnish conditions of possibility of all knowledge of objects' (ibid. A89-90/B122).

The problem was especially urgent for Kant because he believed that the propositions of mathematics and physics possess a universal validity which cannot be justified by induction, that is, by generalization from the observed to the unobserved; for example, from the fact that we have only seen black crows to the universal proposition applicable to the whole of space and time that 'All crows are black'. Hume had argued, and Kant agreed, that induction could not provide certain knowledge: no universal proposition may be legitimately inferred from a set of particular propositions, however many members that set may have. At the same time, Kant rejected Leibniz's claim that the sciences were 'truths of reason', whose denial entails a contradiction. Such a truth, he argued, can only be an analytical judgement such as 'All bodies are extended', where the predicate is already contained in the sense of the subject and where therefore the sentence is true by virtue of the meaning of the words it contains. Kant considered mathematics and physics to be based on *synthetic* judgements, which do not merely unpack the meaning of the subject of the sentence, but tell us something new about it. But the propositions of the sciences are also necessary; in other words, they possess universal validity. They cannot, therefore, be discovered *a posteriori*, by means of observation and the accumulation of experience. Hence, 'the proper problem of pure reason is contained in the question: How are *a priori* synthetic judgements possible?' (Ibid. B19.)

Kant's answer to this question is the starting-point of German classical idealism. Having distinguished the passive faculty of sensibility, where intuitions (sense-impressions) are registered, from the active one of understanding, he tried to base the validity of arithmetic and geometry on their relation to time and space respectively, which he considered to have no absolute reality, but rather to be the *a priori* forms of intuition, providing part of the framework of possible experience. Similarly, the objective, causally governed world of common sense, and of Newtonian physics does not exist independently of the conditions of possible experience, but is transcendentally ideal, constructed from the categories of the understanding. Kant's attempt to prove this claim, the transcendental deduction of the categories, is the corner-stone of the *Critique of Pure Reason*. Central to it is an analysis of judgement. 'Just as sensibility is the faculty of intuitions,' Kant writes, 'so the understanding is the faculty of thinking, that is, of bringing the presentations of the senses under rules.'[7] It does so by means of judgements, in which particular impressions are subsumed under concepts: 'all judgements are functions of unity among our representations.' (*CPR* A69/B93-4.) Understanding consists, then, in synthesis, 'the act of putting different representations together, and of grasping what is manifold in them in one knowledge' (ibid. A77/B103). Hume was right to deny that objective connections are given in sense-experience: these depend upon the subsumption of intuitions under concepts, in other words, their combination or synthesis, which 'cannot be given through objects' and is 'an act of the self-activity of the subject' (ibid. B130). Yet the judgements involved in such syntheses cannot be what Kant calls reflective, merely generalizing from past experience, for then the very possibility of coherent, stable, and continuous experience would be in question, threatening from moment to moment to disintegrate into a chaos of unrelated sense-impressions: 'unity of synthesis according to empirical concepts would be altogether accidental, if these latter were not based on a transcendental ground of unity. Otherwise it would be possible for appearances to crowd in upon the soul, and yet be such as would never allow of experience.' (Ibid. A111.)

This 'transcendental ground of unity' on which the possibility of experience depends can only have its source in the subject.

Kant was, however, careful to distinguish the *transcendental subject* from the empirical self of which we seem to be aware when thinking, perceiving, dreaming and so on. Hume had already denied to this latter, Cartesian self any unity, reducing it to 'nothing but a bundle or collection of different perceptions, which succeed one another with an inconceivable rapidity, and are in a perpetual flux and movement'.[8] Kant's subject, the 'transcendental unity of apperception', is not given in experience, but underlies it, rendering it possible. Unless every intuition can be referred to an enduring self, presupposed by, but not present in, sense-experience, then even this experience, the Humean flux of impressions, let alone the Newtonian physical world, would be impossible: 'it must be possible for the "I think" to accompany all my representations; for otherwise something would be represented in me which could not be thought at all, and that is equivalent to saying that the representation would be impossible, or at least would be nothing to me.' (Ibid. B131-2.)

The point of this argument was to permit Kant to ground the objectivity of the empirical world, and of the sciences that depict it, although not as a realm of being existing independently of the subject. Rather, its objectivity arises from the fact that 'in original apperception everything must necessarily conform to the conditions of the thoroughgoing unity of self-consciousness, that is, to the universal functions of synthesis' (ibid. A111-12). The transcendental unity of apperception involves applying to the manifold of intuition (the flux of sense-impressions) twelve categories, derived from the logical form of the judgement. Kant went on to try to show that the normal, everyday world of objects and causes arises from the subsumption of sense-impressions under these categories. Thus, 'universal laws of nature have their ground in our understanding, which prescribes them to nature'.[9] Their universality depends on their applicability to every possible experience: thus, the possibility of synthetic *a priori* judgements is established, their validity deriving not from their success in mirroring the inner structure of being, but from the synthesizing activities of the transcendental subject. Reality other than in the form given to us through the interaction of the human faculties of sensibility and understanding is an unknowable thing-in-itself; Kant sought to show in the 'Transcendental Dialectic', the third main section of the *Critique of Pure Reason*, that reason falls into 'transcendental illusion', for example, certain irresoluble antinomies, once it seeks knowledge outside the boundaries of possible experience.

Kant's subordination of the public, objective world of common-sense realism and the inner world of the Cartesian self to the activity of a transcendental subject laid the basis of Hegel's absolute idealism. Already in Fichte, Kant's distinctions between appearance and thing-in-itself, subject and object, theoretical and practical reason had become secondary and relative. Primary instead was the activity of the 'I', which creates the objective world by positing a 'not-I' opposed to itself. Once disrupted, the original self-identity of the 'I' gives way to an infinite process in which one opposition succeeds another, every synthesis being only temporary, no sooner attained than overthrown by a new antithesis. The unity of subject and object, thought and action becomes the unattainable goal of what Hegel would call a 'bad infinity', an endless striving which can never regain the self-identity which it has lost. Schelling took a step further. The 'I' that is the original unity of being prior to all oppositions became the Absolute Idea, transcending any individual subject, and representing the ultimate identity of God and his creation. But Schelling's Absolute is ineffable, knowable not by rational, discursive means, but only intuitively, 'absolute indifference, . . . a unique being apart from all antitheses, in which all distinctions break up . . . [having] no predicates save lack of predicates'[10] – 'the night in which . . . all cows are black', as Hegel sardonically put it.[11]

Hegel, like the Neoplatonists, Spinoza, and Schelling before him, sought to show that God and the world are identical. What makes him unique is that, first, he attempted to realize this project, not through the abandonment of conceptual reasoning, but rather by revealing what he believed to be its inner structure, and, secondly, where his predecessors had tended to resolve individual subjects into the Absolute, Hegel continued to accord central importance to the concept of subjectivity as it had evolved in Western philosophy from Descartes to Kant.

The bizarre blend of rationalism and Neoplatonism character-istic of Hegel's thought emerges clearly at the beginning of *The Science of Logic*, whose '*realm is the Truth as it is, without husk in and for itself . . . God as he is in his eternal essence before the creation of Nature and of a Finite Spirit*' (GL i. 60). Hegel rejected Kant's conception of logic as the 'science of the mere form of our intellectual cognition' but 'not in any way of its *matter*'.[12] For Hegel, 'the form is the indwelling process of the concrete content itself.'[13] The categories of Logic do not merely provide the framework within which our empirical knowledge is organized, but are the moving forces within reality itself. The structure of the *Logic* is that of the process through which the forms of thought, the most general and abstract categories, acquire a content by evolving it out of themselves; this structure reveals the pattern through which the Absolute Idea alienates itself in the external realm of nature before attaining to full consciousness of itself in Absolute Spirit. Its starting point is the original dumb unity of Being, the most basic of categories, whose complete lack of any specific quality, like Schelling's 'absolute indifference', renders it identical to Nothing. But the self-negation of Being is also the means through which it acquires a determinate content. For Hegel, negation does not simply cancel that which it negates, it is rather *determinate* negation, which absorbs the cancelled category within a new unity, providing the impulse to move from one category to another. It is only, moreover, by virtue of negation that Being acquires a content; the definite shape and character possessed by any entity depends upon the contrast between it and what it is not, the barrier it sets up between itself and others.

The differentiation of Being is also its self-estrangement, a process which is at its most extreme in the sphere of Essence (Book II of the *Logic*), where the interdependence of the different aspects of reality is recognized, but their inner connection not grasped. The doctrine of Essence embraces such categories as essence and appearance, cause and effect, form and content; it is the realm of 'reflective understanding, which, while it assumes the differences to possess a footing of their own, and at the same time also expressly affirms their relativity, still combines the two statements, side by side, or one after the other, by an "also", without bringing these thoughts into one, or unifying them into the notion.' (*LL* 166.) It was Kant especially that Hegel had in mind here – the former's stress on the limits of reason, and insistence that any attempt to penetrate beneath the appearances to things-in-themselves would lead only to irresoluble antinomies. Hegel denounced Kant's hostility to contradiction, expressive of 'the customary tenderness for *things*', which treats contradiction as 'an accident, a kind of abnormality or paroxysm of sickness which will soon pass away' (*GL* ii. 50, 67). From the standpoint of speculative reason, however, 'all things are *contradictory in themselves*' and 'negativity . . . is the inherent pulsation of self-movement and liveliness' (ibid. ii. 66, 69). Determinate negation does not simply introduce difference into the original unity of Being: at the third, speculative stage of the *Logic*, the doctrine of the Notion, negation, as the negation of the negation, breaks down the barriers between the determinations that have evolved in the sphere of Essence, bringing to consciousness their inner unity. In doing so, negation realizes the programme of absolute idealism: the apparently stable, self-subsistent, finite entities making up the material world are shown to be contradictory, possessing identity not in themselves but as manifestations of the Absolute. 'The absolute is just because the finite is self-contradictory opposition – just because it is *not*.' (Ibid. ii.70; see also i.68.)

The path taken by the *Logic* – Being/Essence/Notion – is that of subjectivity explored by Hegel in *The Phenomenology of Mind*. Self-consciousness is impossible in the mute unity of Being. The self can only become aware of itself once it has distinguished itself from, and set itself up against another. But this estrangement of the subject from the object, or from other subjects, of necessity gives rise to the 'unhappy consciousness', at odds with itself and with the world. Only when it is grasped as *self*-estrangement, when the subject sees the object as *its* other, as *itself*, posited in opposition to itself only in the course of its own formation, can consciousness be at home in the world. Subjectivity is identical with the process through which the original unconscious unity is broken down and transformed into self-estrangement, only to be restored as a richer, higher unity, comprehending the whole of reality as the manifestation of consciousness. It describes a circle, which is the same as that around which the *Logic* revolves. The Notion, which is the negation of the negation, the cancellation of the opposites characteristic of the understanding, involves the restoration of the unity of Being, but at the pinnacle of self-consciousness, embracing all the determinations generated in the course of the *Logic*. The negation of the negation 'is the innermost and most objective moment of Life and Spirit, by virtue of which a subject is personal and free' (ibid. ii. 478). The subject which emerges at the end of the *Logic* is not, however, a person, whether finite or infinite, but a structure, the Absolute Idea, identical to the process through which it has been attained. 'In its essential nature the truth is subject: being so, it is merely the dialectical movement, this self-producing course of activity, maintaining its advance by returning back into itself'.[14] Thus, 'the Science is a cycle, returning upon itself, where the first is also last and the last first' (ibid. i. 83), while 'the content of the Absolute idea is the whole breadth of ground which has passed under view up to this point' (*LL* 293). The Absolute achieves full self-consciousness in philosophy, which is the recollection (*Erinnerung* – internalization) of the path travelled by the Idea prior to that moment, where the absolute identity of subject and object, thought and reality, God and the world, is conceptually grasped and comprehended. It follows that there can be no sharp distinction made between the philosophical doctrines espoused by Hegel – absolute idealism – and the means whereby they are established. In other words, the opposition between Hegel's dialectical method and his idealistic system drawn first by the young Hegelians and later by Engels cannot be sustained: 'the form is the indwelling process of the concrete content itself.' We shall pursue this issue, central to the problem of Marx's relation to Hegel, in the next two chapters. In the mean time, we must take note of a very different philosophical tradition.

(2) From Kant to Frege

Analytical philosophy is often characterized in terms of its method, the analysis of linguistic usage to clarify or resolve philosophical problems; but, as we shall see, underlying this approach is the assumption that human thought (and the world reflected in that thought) cannot be understood separately from its expression in language. Thought, in other words, is shifted from the private world of the Cartesian self to the public world of discourse. This move, and the peculiar conception of language associated with it, have their origins in certain distinctively Kantian problems. 'Analytical philosophy is post-Fregean philosophy,' writes Michael Dummett.[15] Gottlob Frege's reconstruction of logic was motivated by his desire to vindicate the objectivity and *a priori* truth of mathematics against the psychologism prevalent among the naturalistic materialists dominant in mid-nineteenth-century German philosophy. On the latter view (also found in John Stuart Mill's *System of Logic*, a continuation of the classical empiricism of Locke and Hume, which was subjected to devastating criticism by Frege in *The Foundations of Arithmetic* (1881)), mathematics consisted of inductive generalizations from observation explicable by means of an empirical study of the workings of the human mind. Concerned, like Kant before him, to refute this 'physiology of the understanding' which denied to mathematics any universal validity, Frege argued that the propositions of arithmetic could be derived from the laws of logic alone. Arithmetic is not, as Kant had claimed, synthetic *a priori*, its validity restricted to the realm of possible experience and deriving from the peculiar constitution of the human mind; rather, we can, merely by inference from the laws of logic, establish the truth of arithmetic. Logic does not, then, consist of uninformative analytic truths, since it permits us to discover a very important fact about the world, namely the existence of numbers.

To vindicate this very ambitious claim Frege was compelled to reshape logic in his *Begriffschrift* (1879), which marked the commencement of the modern history of the discipline, containing the essentials of first-order elementary logic. This enormous technical achievement involved a characteristically Kantian starting point. Logic has, since its inception in antiquity, been concerned with valid inference, in other words, with the conditions in which one is entitled to derive a sentence from others. This focus on the relation between sentences is obscured in traditional Aristotelian logic, which is divided into three parts: the doctrine of terms, of judgements, and of syllogisms. The starting point of logic was provided by the constituent terms of a judgement, or sentence, based on its grammatical division into subject and predicate. As Hans Sluga puts it, 'the viewpoint of [Aristotelian] subject-predicate logic was essentially aggregative. It saw the judgement as formed by aggregation out of previously given constituent concepts.'[16] The result was an inability to account for the *combinatorial* character of sentences, the peculiar internal unity they appear to possess. To quote Dummett, 'it then appears problematic how sentences succeed in actually *saying* anything, true or false, for the sentence has appeared to degenerate into a list.'[17] Before Frege it was Kant who broke most emphatically with this aggregative approach to logic, treating judgements as syntheses of sense-impressions whose unity precedes, and makes possible the application of the concepts they contain.

Frege made the primacy of sentences fundamental to his reconstruction of logic. 'In Aristotle . . ., the logically primitive activity is the formation of concepts by abstraction, and judgement and inference enter in through an immediate or indirect comparison of concepts via their extensions. . . . As opposed to this, I start out from judgements and their contents.'[18] The *Begriffschrift* commences with the propositional calculus, where the logically permissible combinations of sentences are characterized in terms of the truth-value (truth or falsity) of the constituent sentences. Frege's treatment of the predicate calculus, where he deals with the structure of quantified sentences (those bound by the operators 'all' or 'some'), similarly takes the sentence as basic: rejecting the surface division of sentences into subject and predicate as misleading, he formed predicates from sentences by the omission of one or more occurrences of a singular term; so that, for example, the predicate '. . . is blue', is constructed by removing the singular term 'The sky' from the sentence 'The sky is blue'. This move enabled Frege to develop an analysis of universal propositions which resolved problems which had troubled logicians since the middle ages.[19]

Frege's 'logicist' programme of reducing arithmetic to logic foundered on the paradox of set theory discovered by Bertrand Russell. His recasting of logic, however, survived the crash and was taken over by Moore and Russell in Cambridge at the turn of the century, by the logical positivists of Vienna, and by the ordinary language philosophers of Oxford between the wars. The new logic became in their hands a key to the understanding, and sometimes the criticism of natural languages. Frege himself had only been peripherally interested in this question, since he believed that the inferential patterns and conceptual structures revealed by his logical notation could only be imperfectly expressed in ordinary language. For example, 'the King of France is bald' is a perfectly acceptable sentence of natural language, even though the fact that its subject has no referent (there is no King of France) deprives the sentence of a truth-value according to Frege's analysis of proper names, and therefore violates the logical law that every sentence must be either true or false. Analytical philosophers have characteristically sought either to improve on natural language, to 'regiment' it so that it can fit what Donald Davidson called 'the Procrustean bed' of logic,[20] or to explore the workings of ordinary language, denying the possibility of such a regimentation.

A classic instance of this first approach is Russell's theory of descriptions, where he offered an alternative analysis of sentences such as 'The King of France is bald', showing that their surface grammatical structure can be replaced by a logically acceptable, because false (rather than truth-valueless), existential statement – in this case, 'There is one and only one person who is the King of France, and he is bald'.[21] P. F. Strawson's celebrated defence of Frege's analysis sought to reinstate the validity of ordinary usage reflected in the surface structure of subject-predicate sentences: 'Neither Aristotelian nor Russellian rules give the exact logic of any expression of ordinary language; for ordinary language has no exact logic.'[22]

Both approaches none the less have much in common. As Richard Rorty puts it, 'the only difference between Ideal Language Philosophers [the theorists of 'regimentation'] and Ordinary Language Philosophers is a disagreement about which language is Ideal.'[23] Both schools share the presumption that the resolution of philosophical problems turns on ascertaining the 'logical form' of linguistic expressions. And whatever their views on the nature of 'logical form', analytical philosophers tend to share a Fregean conception of language, in at least two important respects. First, Frege distinguished between the sense and reference of expressions. An expression's reference is the extra-linguistic entity it designates – in the case of singular terms, for example, abstract or concrete objects. The reference of expressions is, however, determined by their sense, the 'mode of presentation' of the reference.[24] As Dummett puts it, the 'sense of a word thus consists in the means by which a reference of an appropriate kind is determined for that word'.[25] In line with Frege's anti-psychologism, 'the sense of a word has nothing to do with any propensity to call up mental images in the mind of the hearer and is something wholly objective'.[26] Even where they have rejected Frege's doctrine that the sense of a sentence is given by its truth-conditions, analytical philosophers have generally sought to base their investigation of logical form on a theory of sense.[27]

Analytical philosophy of language has tended to follow Frege in a second respect, summed up in the famous slogan, 'Never ask for the meaning of a word in isolation, but only in the context of a proposition.'[28] Properly understood, this doctrine does not amount to a denial of meaning to words. On the contrary, our ability to make or understand utterances which we have never heard or thought of before depends on there being a pre-existing stock of words which may be combined in new, and unanticipated permutations to form sentences. Rather, the doctrine involves the claim that the meaning (i.e. sense and reference) of words consists in the role they play in determining the meaning of sentences. From the standpoint of a theory of sense, sentences enjoy explanatory primacy. Such an approach is radically at odds with the atomistic conception of language encouraged by the traditional logic, starting as it did with 'the independently significant elements provided by simple apprehension . . . [known] variously as "ideas", "notions", "impressions", "sensations" or "concepts"'.[29] On this conception, the meanings of words are determined individually, and they are identical to the extra-linguistic objects to which they refer. A version of this was present in Locke, and it was still at work in the logical atomism of Russell and the early Wittgenstein: thus, for the latter the sense of a sentence is nothing other than its depiction of a possible arrangement of atomic objects.

There are, therefore, important points of contact between the picture of language prevalent among analytical philosophers and certain themes in Kant, in particular, anti-atomism, the priority of judgements over concepts, and anti-psychologism, the objectivity of logic, its irreducibility to a causal account of the empirical genesis of beliefs. Moreover, as Sluga points out,

> The Fregean or analytic understanding is foreshadowed in Kantian formalism. . . . Kant alone [of the German idealists] had insisted on the separation of form and content, consigning the content of human knowledge once and for all to empirical science and redefining philosophy as the *a priori* forms of human understanding.[30]

The differences, however, are as important as the similarities. As we saw, for Kant, the unity of the judgement depends on the existence, underlying the empirical self and its experience, of a transcendental subject. Thus, 'a judgement is the presentation of the unity *of consciousness* of several presentations.'[31] Analytical philosophy, despite the priority accorded to sentences in its account of language, does not similarly presume the synthesizing activities of a transcendental subject. Wittgenstein's celebrated argument against the possibility of a private language in the *Philosophical Investigations*, although sometimes compared with

Kant's transcendental deduction of the categories, is surely profoundly destructive of such a subject, since it seeks to prove that our notion of a self, and our ability to describe its experience are parasitic upon the existence of a public language. If the argument works, language is autonomous of any subject, pure or empirical. Wittgenstein writes elsewhere in terms very close to Frege's anti-psychologism: 'the psychological processes which are found by experience to accompany sentences are of no interest to us. What does interest us is the understanding that is embodied in an explanation of the sense of a sentence.' But such an explanation can only be given by another sentence. 'One can say that meaning drops out of language; because what a proposition means is told by yet another proposition.'[32]

Language thus is sufficient to itself. Any attempt to explain it from a vantage point outside discourse is doomed to failure: the search for an extra-linguistic meaning leads only to the proliferation of new sentences. The Fregean principles of the objectivity of sense, and the explanatory primacy of sentences seem to have led, no doubt contrary to Frege's own intentions, to the constitution of an autonomous realm of sentences. We shall return to this view of language, and its analogies with the French post-structuralist 'revolution of language' in Chapters 5 and 6.[33] Let us content ourselves for the moment with noting that it helps to explain the analytical tradition's peculiar conception of philosophical method. Rorty sums this up as 'methodological nominalism',

> the view that all questions philosophers have asked about concepts, subsistent universals, or 'natures' which (a) cannot be answered by empirical enquiry concerning the behaviour or properties of particulars subsumed under such concepts, universals or natures and (b) which can be answered in *some* way, can be answered by answering questions about the use of linguistic expressions and in no other way.[34]

In the light of this thesis, we can understand analytical philosophers' interest in the formulation of a theory of sense, for such a theory would greatly facilitate, perhaps render possible, the investigation of the logical form of particular expressions or classes of expressions.

Methodological nominalism, the belief that such investigations hold the key to traditional philosophical problems about the nature of reality, the foundations of knowledge, the status of ethics and so on, is particularly associated with Wittgenstein and Oxford ordinary language philosophy. Thus the former believed that philosophical problems arose from misunderstandings of how language worked, and could, therefore, not be solved, but only dissolved, dissipated by a description of the 'depth grammar' of particular expressions. But even those philosophers who, under the influence of Russell and the Vienna Circle, do not share this tenderness for ordinary language, seek its reform with the same end in view. Quine, for example, arch-opponent of ordinary language philosophy, justifies his strategy by the 'unswerving conviction that logical regimentation . . . was of the essence of the *clarification of meaning'*.[35] Different theories of sense subserve the same aim, the resolution of philosophical problems by the analysis of language. This is particularly clear in the case of Donald Davidson, author of the most ambitious attempt to construct a theory of sense based on the apparatus of formal logic. One of his papers on broader philosophical issues is called 'The Logical Form of Action Sentences', another begins with the question, 'What is the logical form of singular causal statements . . . ?'[36]

This belief, shared by analytical philosophers, despite their other differences, that philosophical issues are to be resolved through the analysis of meaning, is comparatively easy to understand when we see underlying other doctrines the belief that language is no mere translucent medium connecting our minds and the world, but rather is the very stuff of our thought, from the most intimate of personal experiences to the complex, articulated systems of mathematics and the natural sciences. Such a belief is implied by Wittgenstein's private language argument and by Gilbert Ryle's attack on the Cartesian concept of mind as a 'ghost in a machine',[37] but it is expressed in many other forms. Thus Quine is led to a similar view by his behaviourist rejection of 'a pernicious mentalism' which treats 'a man's semantics as somehow determinate in his mind beyond what might be implicit in his dispositions to overt behaviour'; by contrast, 'when a naturalistic philosopher turns himself to the philosophy of mind, he is apt to talk of language.'[38] Analytical philosophy, beyond its internal differences, can be seen as part of that broad movement in twentieth-century Western culture which in philosophy, literature, and the arts has seen language turn back upon itself, becoming, at the extreme, not the point of contact between the Cartesian self and the world, but *the* self and *the* world. Some of the implications of this 'revolution of language' will be explored in other chapters.

2. The End of Philosophy?

(1) The Discovery of the Proletariat

It was probably inevitable that Marx should have started out a philosopher.[1] The famous letter to his father of 10 November 1837 in which Marx announced his conversion to Hegelian philosophy recorded an experience undergone by many German intellectuals of his generation. Even the unspeculative Engels, later to grow impatient with Marx's jousts with the young Hegelians, travelled much the same path.[2] Hegelianism, promoted by Altenstein, the Prussian Minister of Education and Culture, enjoyed the virtual status of an official philosophy in the 1820s and 1830s; however, it contained tensions which help to explain why Hegel's thought provided one of the main starting points for radical criticism of the German status quo in the 1840s.

Philosophy occupied a peculiar position within Hegel's system, standing as it did at the culminating point of the entire process of development, and reconstructing this process in retrospect as Absolute Spirit's attainment of self-consciousness. The contradictions which provide the motor of this evolution are resolved *post festum*, rationalized after the event by the philosopher as necessary steps in the journey to absolute knowledge. 'Philosophy is thus the true theodicy,' Hegel wrote, and its history 'the world's history in its innermost signification.'[3] In Karl Löwith's words, for Hegel 'philosophy as a whole represents the same reconciliation with reality as does Christianity through the incarnation of God; as the finally comprehended reconciliation, it is philosophical theology.'[4] But if it therefore fell to philosophy to reveal the thoroughgoing identity of the Absolute Idea and reality, there remained some slack within Hegel's system, it being to some degree open whether philosophy might play some part in bringing this identity to consciousness by contributing to the transformation of the everyday world. Hegel's early enthusiasm for the French Revolution led him to believe that the *Phenomenology*, completed the night before Napoleon defeated

26

the Prussian army at Jena, was part of the same struggle for human liberation. Indeed, he believed that his work would accomplish more than the practical feats of French arms, writing in 1808 that 'once the realm of notions is revolutionized, actuality does not hold out.'[5] His later political disillusionment led Hegel to conclude that Germany had achieved the emancipation of the human spirit necessary to bring the identity of Idea and reality to consciousness at the time of the Reformation. He became an opponent of political reform, declaring that '*what is rational is actual and what is actual is rational*': liberal proponents of change counterposed the Idea to existing reality, lacking the intellectual penetration to grasp that the Absolute had already been realized and was at one with the world.[6]

Hegel's school rapidly polarized after the master's death in 1831 between a right wing which accepted his canonization of the Prussian state as the incarnation of the Idea, and a left wing which demanded that this state should conform to the Idea. The young Hegelians, or 'Hegelings', as the left wing came to be called, began with a critique of religion. Like the French *philosophes* of the eighteenth century they had political as well as philosophical reasons for doing so: the Lutheran Church was one of the main props of Prussian absolutism. They were also encouraged by Hegel's analysis of religion as imperfect, pictorial representations of the deeper, conceptual truths of philosophy. David Strauss's *Life of Jesus* (1835) treated the Bible as the myths of the Jewish people; Bruno Bauer's lengthy series of critiques of the Gospels revealed them to be the inventions of their authors; Ludwig Feuerbach's *The Essence of Christianity* (1841) reduced religion to the alienated expression of the human essence. The Hegelian left was prompted to develop a more explicitly political challenge to the Prussian state, demanding its democratic reform, after the hopes of change raised by the accession to the throne in 1840 of King Friedrich Wilhelm IV were dashed. The new monarch rapidly made plain his hostility to a constitutional monarchy, the talisman of the liberal opposition. Altenstein's successor as Minister of Education and Culture, Eichhorn, summoned Schelling to the chair of philosophy at Berlin to root out the 'dragon seed of Hegelianism'. The ageing idealist's inaugural lectures in November 1841 marked the end of the Prussian state's flirtation with philosophy. To an audience that included Bakunin, Burckhardt, Engels, and Kierkegaard,

Schelling denounced the 'negative-rational' character of Hegel's dialectic, and preached a 'positive philosophy' of acceptance of the 'immemorial, blind existence' that is the world.[7] The more practically minded of the young Hegelians, such as Arnold Ruge, who had previously placed their hopes in what they believed to be the liberal, Protestant traditions of the Prussian state, now began to follow a more radical course.

Left Hegelianism, as it evolved in the face of increasingly ferocious repression, took two main forms. The first, developed by Bruno Bauer and his followers in the Berlin *Doktorklub*, abandoned Hegel's absolute idealism for a position rather similar to the subjective idealism of Fichte, in which the objective world is merely posited by the individual ego in order to attain self-consciousness.[8] Bauer discovered two Hegels, the 'exoteric' public figure, a Christian philosopher of reconciliation with reality, and the 'esoteric' Hegel, a secret atheist. This interpretation, developed at length in Bauer's squib *Die Posaune des Jüngsten Gerichts über Hegel den Atheisten und Antichristen* (1841), treated the Absolute as merely a metaphor for human self-consciousness. Bauer shared Hegel's belief in the omnipotence of spirit, attaching special importance to the latter's critique of those concepts, such as substance and the Kantian thing-in-itself, which suggested the existence of a reality irreducible to thought. At the centre of Bauer's version of Hegelianism was the *Phenomenology*, regarded as a history of the evolving forms of self-consciousness. For Bauer, unlike Hegel, there was no term to the process – history did not culminate in Absolute Spirit, but would continue to infinity, each particular realization of self-consciousness breaking down by virtue of its internal tensions, and giving rise to another.

If Bauer returned to a historicized version of Fichte, Feuerbach's much more radical critique of Hegel amounted to a reversion of the philosophical materialism of the French Enlightenment, to Diderot, Holbach, and La Mettrie. For Feuerbach, the subject of the dialectic was neither the Absolute Idea nor the individual self, but nature, crowned by man, as its highest development.[9] He accepted Hegel's account of the *structure* of the dialectic, the triad of original dumb unity, self-estrangement and ultimate reconciliation. He believed, however, that Hegel's error went much further than a misidentification of the subject of this process, muffling the finite ego in the Absolute Idea. It consisted, rather, in the inversion of subject and predicate. This involved the transformation of thought from a reflection of the empirical world into the essence of reality and of nature, the authentic subject, into a manifestation of the Idea. This speculative feat was, according to Feuerbach, a reflection of an inversion at work in reality itself, man's estrangement from himself: the evolution of human consciousness led to the creation by the imagination of an alien being to whom all man's essential powers were attributed. This impoverishment of man to the profit of a fictional deity had reached its most extreme expression in Christianity. The reconciliation of God and his creation in religion, conceptually comprehended by philosophy, was not, as Hegel had claimed, the attainment of absolute knowledge, but the depths of human alienation. The task of the philosophy of the future, Feuerbach argued, was to demolish those fictions, God and the Absolute, setting in their place man: religion and idealist metaphysics were necessary stages in the development of man's awareness of his own unique identity, his evolution from an original unconscious unity with nature, but now their time was passed. Feuerbach's hostility to idealism went even further. Since man was essentially a natural being, those aspects of him which revealed his dependence on nature, his sense-perceptions and physical needs, provided the only certain source of knowledge. Humanism could only be vindicated by the most thoroughgoing materialism and empiricism.

While Feuerbach's naturalistic materialism was philosophically at odds with Bauer's subjective idealism, their political views were quite similar. Marx later remarked that 'insofar as Feuerbach is a materialist he does not deal with history, and insofar as he deals with history he is not a materialist' (CW 5:41). Like Helvétius and Holbach in the previous century, Feuerbach considered human nature to consist in a fixed number of powers and dispositions which were denied full expression in existing society. The principal obstacle to human emancipation lay in the existence of organized religion, whose power would be destroyed once freedom of thought and speech were established. Bauer broadly agreed, and therefore attached great importance to atheist propaganda. For the young Hegelians generally, history with the Absolute removed was the development of self-consciousness, what Condorcet had called 'the progress of the human mind', the steady, indefinite, and inevitable growth of enlightenment, of man's knowledge of himself and his natural environment. The struggle for political emancipation in Germany could only be a battle of ideas, in which enlightenment would vanquish superstition and reaction.

This idealist philosophy of history was less at odds with Feuerbach's materialism than it might seem at first sight. Galileo, Descartes, and Newton had in the seventeenth century dethroned the Aristotelian conception of the world as a teleological order in which the behaviour of human beings and physical objects was intelligible only in so far as it could be seen to contribute to the overarching purpose. Subsequently, man and the physical universe had been torn apart. Objective reality was identified with matter, with a physical world governed by mechanical laws; man became the Cartesian self, an essentially subjective, mental being. Therefore, the study of man could only consist in the study of the human mind. Thus, the attempts of Hume, Helvétius and others in the eighteenth century to extend the empirical method of physics to the science of man were of necessity psychological rather than social. 'What movement is in the physical universe, passion is in the human,' wrote Helvétius.[10]

Marx's first extant philosophical writings, the doctoral dissertation on Democritus and Epicurus (1841), and his preparatory studies, already reveal a certain dissatisfaction with Bauer's subjectivism, even though the two had been cronies during Marx's time in Berlin at the end of the 1830s. Bauer believed that philosophy and the world were necessarily at odds, since the latter represented thought congealed in a dull material lump, a leaden obstacle to the free activity of spirit; philosophy, therefore, could only take the form of a critique of existing reality. Marx accepted that philosophical systems could only take shape by setting themselves off from the world, creating an 'abstract totality' at odds with the reality from which it had emerged. However, this totality could only be realized, and the Idea translated into actuality by transforming the world in philosophy's image. By doing so, philosophy would abolish itself, turning itself back into the world from which it had broken loose, albeit a changed, rational world. The realization of philosophy consisted in its abolition. Such a resting point would only be temporary: a new system would emerge to challenge reality once again, and so history alternated between periods of inner strife and turmoil and those of rational harmony. While still firmly within a Hegelian framework, viewing philosophy as the moving principle of history, Marx's study of the Greek materialists appears to involve a tacit critique of Bauer's belief that philosophy could only criticize, and not transform the world.[11]

At this point political events pitchforked Marx out of philosophy and into the world. Bauer's dismissal from the theology faculty of Bonn University in March 1842 ended his own hopes of an academic career, and was one of a number of signs that the Prussian government intended to crush all opposition. Marx thereupon joined the staff of the *Rheinische Zeitung*, a newspaper set up by the liberal bourgeoisie of Cologne to press for more enlightened economic policies, but soon taken over by Moses Hess and other young Hegelians, and turned into the Prussian state's most vehement critic. Marx became the paper's editor-in-chief. The experience, which lasted only till the *Rheinische Zeitung's* suppression in March 1843 after constant running battles with the censorship, was of crucial importance in two respects. First Marx rapidly lost patience with the dogmatism, extravagant subjectivism, and rhetorical radicalism of Bauer and his associates, who now called themselves *die Freien* (the free). It was with them in mind that Marx wrote to Arnold Ruge shortly after the collapse of the *Rheinische Zeitung*:

> We do not confront the world in a doctrinaire way with a new principle: Here is the truth, kneel down before it! We develop new principles for the world out of the world's own principles. We do not say to the world: Cease your struggles, they are foolish; we will give you the true slogan of struggle. We merely show the world what it is really fighting for. (*CW* 3:144.)

Already the distance between philosophy and the world is narrowing; the former's task is to bring to consciousness what is at stake in the latter's struggles, not to legislate for them.

The second major development during Marx's time on the *Rheinische Zeitung* was that he 'experienced for the first time the embarrassment of having to take part in discussions on so-called material interests'.[12] Politically Marx was by 1842 'an uncompromising democratic extremist', as Hal Draper puts it, committed to the creation of a Jacobin popular republic.[13] These views were, however, formulated in Hegelian terms. In the *Philosophy of Right* Hegel had attempted to reconcile the vision of society as an organic, harmonious whole (which, especially in his youth, he believed had been realized in the Greek city states of antiquity) with the individual freedom that was the ideological hallmark of the Protestant Reformation. Drawing with great brilliance on Adam Smith, Sir James Steuart, and other political economists, Hegel argued that civil society, the atomistic, competitive world of the market economy, would lead, unless controlled, to economic crises and a dangerous gap between rich and poor. These contradictions could be reconciled only within the framework of the political State, where a harmonious balance would be struck between the organic basis of social life in the family, the demand of the individual subject for moral autonomy, and the dynamic individualism of civil society. The State, then, was the highest form of social reason.

Marx and the other young Hegelians accepted this political philosophy, differing from Hegel chiefly in his identification of the rational State with the contemporary Prussian monarchy. Thus Marx wrote in the *Rheinische Zeitung*: 'recent philosophy . . . looks on the state as the great organism, in which legal, moral and political freedom must be realized, and in which the individual citizen in obeying the laws of the state only obeys the natural law of his own reason, of human reason.' (*CW* 1:202.) This uneasy compromise between Hegelianism and Jacobinism did not survive Marx's experiences as a political journalist in the most highly industrialized part of Germany, and in particular his discovery, while investigating the condition of the Moselle peasantry, and following the Rhenish Estates' debates on legislation penalizing wood thefts, of the close links between the propertied classes, including the *Rheinische Zeitung's* bourgeois backers, and the State. Upon the paper's suppression, he threw himself into a critical examination of Hegel's *Philosophy of Right*.

The resulting manuscript, first published in 1927, is strongly marked by Feuerbach's influence, as are all of Marx's writings of the period 1843-5. Three essays by Feuerbach, 'Necessity of a Reform of Philosophy' (1842), 'Provisional Theses for the Reform of Philosophy' (1842), and *Principles of the Philosophy of the Future* (1843), had a profound impact on the more radical of the young Hegelians, notably Marx, Hess, and Engels. They advocated a materialist humanism, and seemed to imply that man's alienation could only be abolished in a communist society.[14] Feuerbach's socialism was primarily an ethical doctrine, looking forward to an intellectual and emotional conversion that would open men's eyes to their common humanity and see the triumph of love over egoism. His critique of Hegel, however, set Marx on the road to a more materialistic and revolutionary communism. The dominant motif of the *Critique of Hegel's Philosophy of Right* is Hegel's inversion of subject and predicate, reality and thought. Marx argued that the dialectical method did not, as Hegel had claimed, overcome the distinction between the form and content of knowledge, generating the subject-matter of thought from the contradictory movement of the dialectical categories. Rather, Hegel merely took over pre-existing empirical material, turning it into mere exemplifications of the asserted, but unproven identity of the Idea and reality. Rather than comprehending the complexity and diversity of empirical reality, 'the sole interest is in discovering "the idea" pure and simple, the "logical idea", in every element, whether of the state or of nature, and the actual subjects . . . come to be nothing but their mere *names'* (*CW* 3:12). The world is left uncomprehended, reduced to a manifestation of the Absolute. Hegel's philosophy of the State amounts to 'evaporating the existing political definitions into abstract thoughts. Not the logic of the matter, but the matter of logic is the philosophical element. The logic does not serve to prove that state, but the state to prove the logic.' (Ibid. 17-18.) Hegel's 'reconciliation with reality' flows from his method: existing reality is transfigured, transformed into the incarnation of God, and therefore neither criticized nor understood. Hyper-rationalism leads to uncritical positivism.

The critique of Hegel's idealist inversion of subject and predicate, thought and reality, is a prelude to an analysis of the upside-down world which the dialectic reflected. 'Hegel's chief error', Marx wrote, 'is to conceive the *contradiction of appearances as unity in essence, in the idea,* whereas it has something more profound for its essence, namely, an *essential contradiction.'* (Ibid. 91.) The transcendence of contradictions in Hegel's Absolute serves to conceal the real contradictions constitutive of existing society, notably that between civil society and the political State. Far from reconciling the competitive strife of civil society within its harmonious, rational unity, the State is an abstraction from civil society, the product of man's self-estrangement, his division between *bourgeois,* self-seeking individualist, and *citoyen,* member of a political community. Just as, in Christianity, according to Feuerbach, man's species-being, the human essence, is transposed onto an alien being, so it is in the political State, isolated from their real existence in civil society, 'that the individuals of the state are related to themselves as *the essence of the species*' (ibid. 107). Humanity is alienated from itself not only in religion, but in social life, where it exists as a whole only in the delusive unity of the State.

The *Critique of Hegel's Philosophy of Right* marks a major step towards historical materialism by locating the source of alienation in the structure of society rather than the state of man's consciousness. There is, however, little consideration of class-relations, and Marx's politics remain those of 'democratic extremism' rather than communism. Universal suffrage, he wrote, will, by introducing 'true democracy', dissolve the separation between State and civil society, resuming them both back into humanity. But the relation between political institutions and material interests which Marx had brought to light suggested that human emancipation, the abolition of alienation, would involve more than democratic reforms. Such was the theme of the first of Marx's essays in the *Deutsch-Französische Jahrbücher*, a review he jointly edited with Ruge from exile in Paris (only one issue appeared, in March 1844). Marx argued that religion, Bauer's *bête noire*, could not be abolished by a merely political revolution, as the influence of Christianity in the US showed, but, as the product of a more fundamental estrangement, would survive until a *human*, and not merely political, emancipation destroyed the distinction between *bourgeois* and *citoyen*.

This essay, 'On the Jewish Question', in which Marx criticized the limited character of previous, bourgeois revolutions, such as those of 1776 and 1789, took him to the threshold of communism. He crossed it in his second contribution to the *Deutsch-Französische Jahrbücher*, the introduction to his unpublished, and earlier manuscript on the *Philosophy of Right*. Here he returned to the theme of his study of Democritus and Epicurus, the relation between philosophy and the world. The efflorescence of idealist philosophy in Germany, Marx argued, arose from the country's wretchedly backward state: 'in politics the Germans *thought* what other nations did.' (Ibid. 180.) Philosophy, in its propensity to invert subject and predicate, thought and reality, reflects the self-estranged society which denies and alienates the human essence. At the same time, by presenting an image of a world in which alienation has been overcome, philosophy contains the aspiration to transform the world. Against those, perhaps the communist secret societies, who ignored philosophy, Marx argued that '*you cannot supersede philosophy without making it a reality*', without, in other words, bringing into existence the harmonious society of which the Absolute is a distorted picture; at the same time, he told the young Hegelians, you cannot '*make philosophy a reality without superseding it*', by abolishing the alienated society from which it arose (ibid. 181). The Idea and reality can be made identical only by transforming reality, an act which, by creating a rational world, will make redundant the vision of such a world, in the extraterrestrial form of the Idea, nurtured by German idealism. Such a transformation would require a '*radical* revolution', no mere second edition of 1789; it could only be accomplished by the proletariat, 'a class with *radical chains*', whose condition amounted to 'the *complete loss* of man' (ibid. 184, 186). Significantly, at the very moment when he first espoused the cause of the working class, Marx looked ahead to the end of philosophy.

(2) The Formation of Historical Materialism

The 1843 'Introduction', although Marx's first text as a revolutionary communist, marked only the beginning of an intellectual and political journey which was to culminate in *Capital*. At this stage the proletariat was not yet a determinate class (formed within specific relations of production which endow it with the capacity to create a classless society) but still, in Auguste Cornu's words, 'a little like the protagonist of the Feuerbachian drama of man's destiny, like the incarnation of humanity which, fallen to the depths of alienation, draws, from the very extremes of its dispossession, the reason and motive for the re-appropriation of its alienated essence'.[15]

More important, Marx was still enough of a young Hegelian to regard the proletariat as, in his own words, the '*passive* element', the '*material* basis' of the German revolution, an inert mass awaiting the spark of philosophy, so that 'the *emancipation of the human being*' will be the work of an alliance whose '*head* . . . is philosophy, its *heart* . . . the *proletariat*' (CW 3:183, 187). The metaphor of 'head' and 'heart' is borrowed directly from Feuerbach's 'Provisional Theses', where the terms refer, respectively, to German idealism and French materialism, the alliance of which Feuerbach hoped would provide the basis of 'real humanism'. It depends for its force on the Hegelian contrast between spirit – the principle of activity, universality, and change – and matter – passive, atomistic, self-seeking. Applied to the relation of philosophy to the proletariat, the contrast could only serve to encourage the elitist attitude expressed by another Feuerbachian communist, Engels, at much the same time: 'with the philosophers to think, and the working men to fight for us, will any earthly power be strong enough to resist our progress?' (CW 4:236.) Bauer and the Freien, frustrated by their political impotence, took this elitism to extremes, denouncing the masses as the barrier to all progress, an inert, reactionary obstacle to the activity of spirit. But when Ruge, in line with this attitude, dismissed the Silesian weavers' uprising of 1844 as insignificant, Marx sprang to their defence. In his reply to Ruge, written in August 1844, no longer is philosophy the active element; rather, 'it is only in the proletariat that it [the German people] can find the dynamic element of its emancipation' (CW 3:202).

Behind this shift towards treating the working class as the active force in the revolutionary process lay Marx's arrival in Paris in October 1843. His stay there lasted only fifteen months, but it was of seminal importance. Paris, Walter Benjamin's 'capital of the nineteenth century', was then the centre of an extraordinary efflorescence of socialist and communist theories and organizations, in a country ruled by a narrow clique of bankers and courtiers, undergoing rapid industrial development, and already shaken by several major working-class revolts.[16] Amid this whirlpool, three very important things happened to Marx. First, he encountered the German and French communists. There were some 40,000 German immigrants in Paris in 1844, the overwhelming majority of them artisans. Among them the League of the Just, driven underground for its role in the abortive 1839 insurrection of Blanqui and the Société des Saisons, exercised a growing influence. Marx's contacts with this group, whose ideas were a mixture of the Utopian socialism of Fourier, the social Christianity of Lamennais, and the conspiratorial putschism of Blanqui, and his contacts with their French counterparts, were his first experience of working-class organization. The impact was profound. 'You would have to attend one of the meetings of the French workers', he wrote to Feuerbach in August 1844, 'to appreciate the pure freshness, the nobility, which burst forth from these toil-worn men.' (*CW* 3:355.) Secondly, Marx's commitment, emotional as well as intellectual, to the cause of the working class was further reinforced by his meeting with Engels when the latter visited Paris at the end of that same month. This began the partnership which was to end only with Marx's death. Engels, who had been working for his family's firm in Manchester since the end of 1842, brought to this alliance his personal experience of Chartism, the first mass proletarian movement of the nineteenth century, combined with a direct acquaintance with the horrors of the Industrial Revolution which he was soon to document in *The Condition of the Working Class in England*. Thirdly, as Marx was later to put it, his *Critique of Hegel's Philosophy of Right* had led him to conclude that 'legal relations' and 'political forms . . . originate in the material conditions of life, the totality of which Hegel, following the example of English and French thinkers of the eighteenth century, embraces within the term "civil society"; that the anatomy of this civil society has, however, to be sought in political economy.'[17] During his stay in Paris, Marx threw himself into a study of the classical political economists; he also investigated the class struggles during the great French Revolution.

The result of Marx's first encounter with Smith, Ricardo, and the other economists was the *Economic and Philosophic Manuscripts of 1844*, only published in full in 1932, long after Marx's death. Here Marx outlined a distinctive new conception of human nature essentially at odds with that of Feuerbach, although this only became clear subsequently, in the 'Theses on Feuerbach' and *The German Ideology*. The concept of species-being (*Gattungswesen*), central to Feuerbach's philosophy, has strongly Hegelian overtones. Membership of the human species is not objectively given independently of thought; it evolves as man's consciousness of himself expands. Species-being, the human essence, flowers fully only when man comes to realize intellectually and emotionally his unity with nature and with his fellow men. Feuerbach thus preserved a Hegelian conception of history as the evolution of forms of consciousness; man's self-estrangement in religion is a necessary prelude to the establishment of the unity of subject and object. However, this unity is that of man and nature, not of the Idea and its empirical manifestations. It is man who is the culmination of history, his species-being fully developed, rendered explicit as consciousness of his humanity, and of his roots in nature.

Marx took over the concept of species-being, giving it a new content. Feuerbach's conception of man as a sensuous and needy being implied a basically passive relationship to the world. (One of his key concepts, *Sinnlichkeit*, denotes both the sensible natural world and sensibility, the receptive faculty which, according to Kant, registers sense-impressions prior to their transformation into experience by the understanding.)[18] For Marx, by contrast, man is defined by his essentially active relation to his environment. This claim is expressed most clearly in the first thesis on Feuerbach: 'The chief defect of all previous materialism (that of Feuerbach included) is that things, reality, sensuousness are conceived only in the form of the *object, or of contemplation,* but not as *sensuous human activity, practice,* not subjectively.' (*CW* 5:3.) This 'sensuous human activity' is labour, as Marx makes clear in the *Manuscripts*:

> It is just in his work upon the objective world . . . that man really proves himself to be a *species-being*. This production is his active species-life. Through this production, nature appears as *his* work and *his* reality. The object of labour is, therefore, the *objectification of man's species-life*: for he duplicates himself no only, as in consciousness, intellectually, but also actively in reality, and therefore he sees himself in a world that he has created. (*CW* 3:277.)

Man's species-being consists, not in his self-consciousness, but in his objective relation to nature, the labour-process which provides the framework of man's interaction with his environment.

Labour for Marx has two especially important dimensions. First, human labour is, as Sidney Hook puts it, 'redirective'.[19] Unlike other animals, man does not relate to his environment through a limited set of activities fulfilling certain fixed needs. His ability to reflect on his own activity, in other words, his self-consciousness, means that man can redirect this activity into new forms designed to achieve new goals. Secondly, human labour is transformative. The relationship between man and nature is a dynamic one involving the transformation of both terms of the relation. Human needs and capacities are not fixed, but change as the labour-process enlarges man's productive powers and creates new desires. 'The history of *industry*', Marx wrote, 'and the established *objective* existence of industry are the *open* book of *man's essential powers*.' (*CW* 3:302.) Similarly, nature is not an immediate *datum* independent of that activity, but is itself transformed by that activity.

It is in terms of this second, transformative aspect of human labour that Marx later criticized Feuerbach's concept of *Sinnlichkeit*, at once the static world given in sense-experience, and man's passive relation to that world. Feuerbach, Marx wrote in *The German Ideology*,

> does not see that the sensuous world around is not a thing directly given for all eternity, remaining ever the same, but the product of industry and the state of society; and indeed [product] in the sense that it is a historical product . . . Even the objects of the simplest 'sensuous certainty' are only given him through social development, industry and commercial intercourse. The cherry tree, like almost all fruit trees, was . . . only a few centuries ago transplanted by *commerce* into our zone and therefore only *by* this definite action of a definite society in a definite age has it become 'sensuous certainty' for Feuerbach. (*CW* 5:39.)

This passage throws light on Marx's remark in the 'Theses on Feuerbach' that 'in contradistinction to materialism, the *active* side was set forth abstractly by idealism' (ibid. 3). It suggests a partial rapprochment with Hegel, recalling the discussion of 'sense-certainty' at the beginning of the *Phenomenology*, where Hegel argued that even the most immediate sense-experience is mediated, is inextricably bound up with universal concepts, and therefore has arisen from an interaction of subject and object rather than, as the classical empiricists and Feuerbach claimed, the passive reception of impressions by the mind. Marx, like Hegel, refused to take the empirically given on its own terms. He agreed that all sense-experience is mediated. But, whereas for Hegel this mediation derives ultimately from the activity of the Notion striving towards full self-consciousness in the Absolute Idea, for Marx it is the result of human labour. It is with this in mind that we must read Marx's remark that 'the only labour which Hegel knows and recognizes is *abstractly mental* labour' (*CW* 3:333). Kant had accorded to the transcendental subject the role of synthesizing form and matter, categories and intuitions. In

Hegel the activity of this subject produces not merely experience, but reality, as the emanation of the Absolute. Marx now attributed the power of actively shaping the material world to human social practice, to labour. Habermas is right, therefore, to say that in Marx 'synthesis no longer appears as an activity of thought, but as one of material production', with the proviso that this production, as Marx makes clear in *Capital*, does not *create* reality, merely transforming some aspect of a pre-given environment.[20]

This conception of human nature as constituted by an active, redirective, transformative relationship to nature through the labour-process is fundamental to Marx's thought. It is the cornerstone of what has been called Marx's 'Prometheanism', his essentially Aristotelian belief that men and women fulfil themselves through the exercise of all their powers, and of his vision of a society in which such self-realization would be possible. Marx discovered this striving towards an integrated, many-sided, dynamic humanity in European literature, in Aeschylus, Shakespeare, Cervantes; like Schiller, Goethe, Hegel, and Heine he attacked the sundered, split mankind of modern Western civilization.[21] He relocated this humanist, aesthetic tradition within a materialist theory of history starting from the labour-process. Much of the *Manuscripts* is devoted to reinterpreting the notion of self-estrangement in the light of this theory. No longer is alienation essentially a mental phenomenon, as in Feuerbach. Capitalist relations of production, as analysed by the classical economists, alienate the worker both from the product of his labour, and from his labour itself. The commodities produced by the worker belong, not to him, but to the capitalist who employs him; labour itself is but a means to an end, a way of staying alive, not man's unique form of self-expression. The alienation of labour, since man's defining characteristic is his active relationship to nature in production, is also the alienation of man from his species-being, from his essence, and therefore his alienation from other men. Only under communism, where alienated labour and its expression in private property are abolished, will human beings be able to enjoy a fulfilled life.[22]

The concept of man involved in Marx's critique of estranged labour underlies his later works. It is to be found, for example, in the discussion in *Capital* of the labour process, 'purposeful activity aimed at the production of use-values', as opposed to exchange-values, 'the universal condition for the metabolic interaction between man and nature, the ever-lasting nature-imposed condition of human existence' (C i. 290). However, the role played by 'human nature' thus conceived shifts between Marx's earlier and latter writings. This point may be clarified by resort to the distinction, made by Popper and his followers, between scientific and metaphysical propositions.[23] A scientific statement may be corroborated or falsified by experience. A metaphysical statement, however, is irrefutable: whether because of its logical form, or simply because its exponents have decided to treat it as irrefutable, such a proposition cannot be shown to be false by observation. Philosophical theories are normally metaphysical; they can never be decisively refuted, and attempts to establish their truth involve some *a priori* procedure, for example, deduction from 'self-evident' principles or conceptual analysis. Metaphysical propositions may, however, function as part of a scientific research programme: here they form part of what Imre Lakatos called the programme's 'heuristic', the set of principles which form the basis on which empirical, falsifiable hypotheses are formulated. In so far as the hypotheses they generate are confirmed or refuted, such metaphysical statements may themselves be regarded as verifiable or falsifiable: thus, Descartes's metaphysical doctrine that matter can only act directly on matter was effectively refuted by the empirical success of the Newtonian research programme involving the concept of action at a distance in the form of the law of universal gravitation.

The Paris *Manuscripts* present us with a metaphysical theory. Marx did not quarrel with Smith and Ricardo's description of capitalism, merely with their interpretation of the facts they uncovered: 'political economy starts with the fact of private property; it does not explain it to us.' (CW 3:270.) Such an explanation required Marx's concept of human nature, and the associated analysis of estranged labour, themselves the result of volatilizing political economy, bringing it into contact with Hegel's dialectic and Feuerbach's theory of alienation. At the end of his discussion of alienation Marx asked: 'How . . . does man come to *alienate*, to *estrange* his labour?' (Ibid. 281.) His answer is at the very end of the *Manuscripts*, in Marx's critique of the Hegelian dialectic. Hegel's merit, according to Marx, is that he 'conceives the self-creation of man as a process, conceives objectification as

loss of the object, as alienation and transcendence of alienation'
(ibid. 332-3). Here Marx took over the characteristic structure of
the Hegelian dialectic, in which the subject can develop only
through self-estrangement and eventual return to itself out of
alienation. Hegel, however, treats the subject of the process as 'a
non-objective, spiritual being' (ibid. 334), while, for Marx,
following Feuerbach, the subject is man, an objective being, part
of a natural, causally governed world. Moreover, objectification,
the transformation of nature by labour, is the most appropriate
expression of the human essence; it is only in certain historically
specific conditions that it becomes estranged labour. Marx's
explanation of why such alienation occurs is, however, Hegelian.
An unalienated existence can occur only if man 'really brings
out all his *species-powers* . . . and treats these powers as objects:
and this, to begin with, is again only possible in the form of
estrangement' (ibid. 333). In other words, alienation is a necessary prelude to the establishment of a truly human society. As
in Hegel, the subject can only become conscious of itself after
a period of internal division, in which its powers are developed in
the form of alien objects; alienation is transcended when the
subject recognizes these objects as its own and resumes them
back into itself, enriched by the diversity it created when
estranged from itself. The structure of the process is the same in
both Marx and Hegel: original unity, self-estrangement,
reconciliation in a higher unity.

At the core of the *Manuscripts* is a teleological philosophy of
history in which the development of social forms is explained by
their role in bringing about the culmination of the historical
process, communism, 'the complete return of man to himself as a
social (i.e. human) being', 'the *genuine* resolution of the conflict
between man and nature and between man and man', 'the riddle
of history solved' which 'knows itself to be this solution' (ibid.
296-7). An explanatory apparatus is provided by Marx's concept
of human nature and by the Hegelian dialectic, in the sense of the
triadic structure through which the subject of history must pass
to realize its full potential. But this concept of human nature, at
the same time as it underlies this philosophy of history, subverts
it. Formally, man plays the same role in the *Manuscripts* as he
does in Feuerbach, providing the basis for a theory of history as
man's passage through alienation. But the *content* of
Gattungswesen has so changed as to prevent it from effectively

playing this role. An account of human nature which denies that there is such a thing as human nature, in the sense of a fixed set of needs and powers, but instead claims that these needs and powers change in response to man's evolving relationship to nature, points toward a theory of history based on the analysis of the historically variable social and technical forms in which production is organized. Indeed, Marx moves decisively towards such a theory in the *Manuscripts*. He had, in earlier writings such as 'On the Jewish Question' and 'Comments on James Mill', analysed capitalism in terms of exchange, treating money as the essential form of alienation; a similar approach was followed at much the same time by Engels in his 'Outlines of a Critique of Political Economy' and Moses Hess in 'Über das Geldwesen'. But the opening sentence of the first of the *Manuscripts* declares that 'wages are determined through the antagonistic struggle between capitalist and worker' (ibid. 235). Here we have the beginnings of an analysis of capitalism in terms of the social relations of production rather than the relations of circulation, a project that would culminate in *Capital*.[24]

Marx was only led consciously to abandon the teleological metaphysic which provide the *Manuscripts* with their theory of historical change after the appearance in late 1844 of Max Stirner's *The Ego and his Own*. This work, in which the subjectivism of Bauer and the *Freien* received its fullest and most extreme expression, is remarkable chiefly for its extension of Feuerbach's critique of Hegel to Feuerbach himself. Reducing reality to the sharp point of the individual ego, Stirner argued that man was, like the Absolute Idea, just another version of God, a form of alienation. Any attempt to subsume the 'I' beneath some essence, some general property in terms of which the 'I' could be explained, was to create an alien and fictional being. 'To know and acknowledge essences alone and nothing but essences, that is religion; its realm is a realm of essences, spooks and ghosts.'[25] To posit essences was not merely idealism; it involved also a denial of the inalienable liberty of the individual ego. 'Every higher essence, such as truth, mankind, and so on, is an essence *over* us.'[26] Only thoroughgoing anarchism, spurning morality, the State, and communism as so many oppressive 'spooks', was compatible with the untrammelled pursuit of its interests by the ego.

Stirner's onslaught may have prompted Marx and Engels to break with Feuerbach. Their first collaborative work, *The Holy*

Family, was written between the completion of the *Manuscripts* and the appearance of *The Ego and his Own* as an attack on the elitism of Bruno Bauer and his brothers (hence the title) from the standpoint of Feuerbachian communism.[27] Then the 'Theses on Feuerbach', written in March 1845, a month after *The Holy Family* was published, declared emphatically: 'Feuerbach resolves the essence of religion into the essence of *man*. But the essence of man is no abstraction inherent in every single individual. In its reality it is the ensemble of social relations.' (*CW* 5:4.) The tension in the *Manuscripts* was thus resolved. Marx's metaphysical theory of human nature henceforth does not play a directly explanatory role. Instead, it provides the philosophical rationale of a scientific research programme whose main concepts, the forces and relations of production, serve to specify the historically variable forms in which social production is organized, and admit of empirical corroboration and refutation via the falsifiable hypotheses they generate. The Feuerbachian concept of species-being is explicitly rejected in *The German Ideology*, written by Marx and Engels in Brussels in 1845-6 in reply to Stirner, but commencing with a lengthy critique of Feuerbach. Here 'On the Jewish Question' and the 1843 'Introduction' are criticized because the break they made with left Hegelianism 'was done in philosophical phraseology' and so 'the traditionally occurring philosophical expressions such as "human essence", "species", etc., give the German theoreticians the desired reason for misunderstanding the real trend of thought' (ibid. 236).

The German Ideology is Marx's and Engels's most vehement, and lengthy (nearly 600 pages) attack on the idealism of the young Hegelians, beginning with a lampoon of 'a valiant young fellow [who] had the idea that men drowned in water only because they were possessed of the *idea of gravity* . . . This valiant fellow was the type of the new revolutionary philosophers in Germany' (ibid. 24). It is also the first systematic presentation of historical materialism. Civil society, 'the form of intercourse determined by the existing productive forces at all previous historical stages, and in its turn determining these, . . . is the true focus and theatre of all history' (ibid. 50). No longer is the burden of explaining historical change taken by the concept of man, filled out by the Hegelian dialectic of self-estrangement and reconciliation. Instead, new concepts, and in particular those of the productive forces, the level of development of man's control over nature, and of the form of intercourse, the social framework within which this control is organized, possess explanatory primacy. Political and cultural forms depend upon the development of civil society. 'It is not consciousness that determines life, but life that determines consciousness.' (Ibid. 37.) German idealism as defended by both old and young Hegelians, in so far as it accords primacy to consciousness over being, is a form of *ideology*, the inverted reflection of material conditions (we shall consider Marx's theory of ideology at some length in Chapter 6 below). Already delineated in *The German Ideology* is a first sketch of the materialist conception of history. Conflicts within civil society, arising from the incompatibility of the existing form of intercourse with the level of development attained by the productive forces, gives rise to class struggle and, eventually, social revolution; the installation of a new ruling class based on different social relations permits the further expansion of man's productive powers.

This theory of historical development underlay Marx's rejection of all attempts to change society by means of enlightenment alone: they must fail since forms of consciousness are not autonomous, but depend upon material conditions. How, then, is social change possible? Marx's answer set him off not only from the young Hegelians, but also from the other socialists of his day. The French Utopians, and especially Fourier, were, like Feuerbach, a continuation of the Enlightenment. Fourier widened the concept of human nature of the *philosophes* to embrace a much broader spectrum of dispositions, desires, and capacities – loving, co-operative, and altruistic as well as individualistic, competitive, and self-seeking; he saw the barrier to human fulfilment as lying, not in superstition, as the *Aufklärer* had thought, but in 'civilization', in bourgeois society itself. But he and the other Utopians shared the conception of history of the *philosophes*: the 'progress of the human mind', continuing to see social change as a product of intellectual enlightenment. If the French socialists championed the cause of the working class, they did so out of sympathy for the latter's suffering, seeing them as not the subject, but the object of social change. Socialism would be introduced *for* the proletariat, not *by* them. Both the revolutionary and reformist wings of French socialism, Blanqui and Dezamy, Fourier and Proudhon, saw change as the work of a small minority acting on behalf of the masses, whether they believed it would be brought about through the armed seizure of power by a communist conspiracy or by peacefully persuading the bourgeoisie that socialism was in their interest. In either case, Marx argued, the result was elitism: the masses were regarded as inert, passive, so moulded by their material circumstances as to be unable to act for themselves. 'The doctrine must, therefore, divide society into two parts, one of which is superior to society.' (Ibid. 4.)

We have seen how Marx adopted such an elitist standpoint in the 1843 'Introduction', treating the proletariat as a mass so wretched that, under the guidance of philosophy, they would leap in one bound from being the negation of humanity to its embodiment. The new materialist conception of history first outlined in *The German Ideology* provided a theoretical basis for its rejection. Workers are led by the exploitative relations of production in which they find themselves to engage in class struggle against their employers. The experience of this struggle transforms their consciousness, encouraging the formation of socialist ideas. 'The coincidence of the changing of circumstances and of human activity or self-change can be conceived and rationally understood only as *revolutionary practice*.' (Ibid.) The education of the masses is not something that can be achieved by an elite 'superior to society' moulding an inert proletariat but is accomplished by the masses themselves as they transform both their own consciousness and society itself in the course of the class struggle. Socialism, in other words, is the *self*-emancipation of the working class: as Marx and Engels were to put it many years later, 'the emancipation of the working classes must be achieved by the working classes themselves.' (SC 307.) This conception of revolutionary consciousness as arising from the interaction between the working class and their objective circumstances was undoubtedly connected to Marx's analysis in the *Manuscripts* of the formation and constant transformation of human nature in the metabolism between man and nature.

The 'Theses on Feuerbach' and *The German Ideology* mark what Louis Althusser called an 'epistemological break' in Marx's thought.[28] For it is only in these works that the implications of Marx's redefinition of 'species-being' in terms of labour are explicitly formulated, and that historical materialism first emerges as a scientific research programme. But what is involved here is more than the replacement of the philosophical teleology of the *Manuscripts* by a new science of social formations; the theory of history contained in the 'Works of the Break' is inextricably bound up with the practical objective of proletarian revolution, serving to specify the material conditions of such a revolution. 'The philosophers have only *interpreted* the world in various ways; the point is to *change* it.' (*CW* 5:5.) Marxism emerged in 1845-6 as the *scientific theory of working-class self-emancipation*.

(3) The Logic of *Capital*

The emergence of historical materialism also involved Marx's and Engels's decisive repudiation of philosophy. Three elements may be isolated in their critique of philosophy. First, there is the theme of texts ranging from Marx's studies of Democritus and Epicurus to the 1843 'Introduction' — philosophy can realize itself only by abolishing itself, by transforming the world in its own image, by giving flesh to the demand for a truly human life. By 1845 this had largely given way to a second argument, which preserves the Feuerbachian conception of philosophy as an inverted reflection of an alienated reality, but treats this as merely one instance of the general relation between forms of consciousness and a society divided into classes. Philosophy, in other words, is ideology. It must be abandoned for empirical science, and in particular for the study of the historically changing 'ensemble of social relations': 'one has to "leave philosophy aside" . . . one has to leap out of it and devote oneself like an ordinary man to the study of actuality.' (Ibid. 236.) There is an almost Comtean ring to the passages of *The German Ideology* which denounce idealist metaphysics in the name of positive science. Thirdly, philosophy stands in for any form of theory. The transformation of social relations does not depend on what Lessing called 'the education of mankind', the spread of enlightenment, but on the involvement of the mass of workers in the class struggle. It is through this *practical* experience, generated from the mainsprings of bourgeois society in the process of production, that a force capable of destroying capitalism and constructing a classless society will emerge. Against especially the German 'true socialists' for whom socialism was an ethical doctrine, a critique of existing society and vision of the future, Marx and Engels insisted that communism was 'the *real* movement which abolishes the present state of things' (ibid. 56).

The new terrain of historical materialism was, however, less rugged and empirical than it first seemed, Marx's and Engels's declarations in *The German Ideology* that, for example, 'the premisses from which we begin are not arbitrary ones, not dogmas, but real premisses . . . the real individuals, their activity and the material conditions of their life' (ibid. 31) contain a large dose of rhetoric that has confused some commentators.[29] Marx no more deduced historical materialism directly from empirical facts than did Newton arrive at the law of gravity by induction from observation. In both cases, new *theories* were formulated as the basis of scientific research programmes: empirical discoveries followed these conceptual advances rather then producing them.[30] We have seen how historical materialism emerged from a philosophical critique of Hegel, Feuerbach, and the *Freien*, and of classical political economy; the formulation of a new metaphysical theory of human nature was a prerequisite of the construction of the fundamental concepts of Marx's theory of history. The rhetoric of 'real premisses' in *The German Ideology* serves primarily to demarcate historical materialism from the young Hegelians, for whom, like their master, the history of philosophy is 'the true theodicy', revealing 'the world's history in its innermost signification'. But Marx's repudiation of German idealism did not guarantee that he had finished with philosophy once and for all; indeed, the further development of historical materialism required him to renew his acquaintance with philosophy, and indeed with Hegel himself.

Contrary to interpretations which treat the versions of historical materialism in *The German Ideology* and *Capital* as identical, the former work suffers from serious conceptual ambiguities, most importantly a persistent confusion of technical and social relations.[31] Of the two most basic concepts of the new science of history, 'productive forces' (*Produktionweise*) involves two elements. The first is what the classical economists called the 'productive powers' of man, the productivity of labour permitted by the existing level of development of technique. Secondly, Marx argued, in line with his stress on the social nature of production, that the technical organization of the labour-process requires a certain 'mode of co-operation' among the producers. This arises from the specific technological imperatives of production, irrespective of tho nature of the prevailing social relations (*CW* 5:43). This analysis of the productive forces presents no serious difficulty, and points toward Marx's discussion of the labour-process in *Capital*, which we shall consider briefly below. The same is not true, however, of the second main concept of *The German Ideology*, 'form of intercourse' (*Verkehrsform*). The meanings of '*Verkehr*' in German include 'traffic', 'transport', 'communication', 'commerce', and 'correspondence'. Marx uses the concept to embrace social relations generally, trade and commerce, along with class and property relations. It is significant that it is the division of labour, embracing both increases in the productivity of labour and changes in the 'form of intercourse', e.g. the creation of a world market, improvements in communications, which is the motor of historical change in *The German Ideology*, whose account of the origins of capitalism is rather similar to Adam Smith's in Book III of *The Wealth of Nations*. Not only, then, does 'form of intercourse' embrace all social relations promiscuously, but it appears to include elements such as the organization of transport which might be regarded more properly as part of the productive forces. Marx, indeed, is led to commit what he would denounce in *Capital* as a cardinal error, confusing the means of production as technical prerequisites of the labour-process with their historically specific social form, capital. (See, for example, ibid. 66.) *The German Ideology* does not, therefore, provide support to those who have sought an interpretation of Marx based on a rigorous distinction between the 'material' (or technical) and 'social' such as to justify treating the development of the productive forces as the source of historical change. The role accorded to the division of labour, which is at once both 'material' and 'social', is symptomatic of a deeper confusion in *The German Ideology*.

Marx resolved this unclarity by introducing, in *The Poverty of Philosophy* (1847), the concept of the *relations of production* (*Produktionsverhältnisse*). These relations are constituted at the level of production; however, they do not, unlike the productive forces, consist in a specific technical organization of the labour-process, but are rather 'social relations based on class antagonism. These relations are not relations between individual, but between worker and capitalist, between farmer and landlord, etc.' (*CW* 6:159.) The concept was further developed in *Capital*, where the forces and relations of production form an articulated unity, the mode of production. The forces of production are analysed in terms of the labour-process, a specific combination of labour, means of production and raw materials, reflecting technical imperatives and permitting a certain level of labour productivity. The labour-process is devoted to the production of use-values which meet specific human needs; as such, it is a feature of every mode of production. Subordinated to capitalist relations of production, and hence to the objective of extracting and accumulating surplus value, the labour-process involves the production of commodities, use-values which at the same time embody specific quantities of value, of socially necessary labour-time.

The relations of production in class societies are 'the specific economic form in which unpaid surplus-labour is pumped out of the direct producers' (C iii. 791). They are, therefore, in the first place, relations *of exploitation*. The mode of appropriation of surplus labour depends upon the specific social form in which the direct producers are combined with the means of production. Thus, the distribution of income depends upon 'the distribution of the instruments of production . . ., which is comprised within the process of production and determines the structure of production. To examine production while disregarding this internal distribution within it is obviously an empty abstraction.' (G 96. See also C ii. 36-7, C iii. 879.) This distribution of the means of production internal to the process of production is prior to, and determines the character of, legal property forms. (See CW 6:197.) It also determines the form of exploitation specific to a given mode of production. In capitalism the direct producers own only their own labour-power, which they must sell to the owners of the means of production in order to survive; in slavery the latter own even labour-power itself; while under feudalism, although the direct producers have some control over the means of production and their own labour-power, the landowner's monopoly of violence and economic power enables him to extract surplus labour from his serfs or tenants.[32]

It is always the direct relationship of the owners of the conditions of production to the direct producers – a relation always naturally corresponding to a definite stage in the development of the methods of labour and thereby its social productivity – which reveals the inner-most secret, the hidden basis of the entire social structure, and with it . . . the corresponding specific form of the state. (C iii. 791.)

It was only with the explicit formulation of the concept of relations of production that historical materialism can be said to be fully constituted. The conceptual structure of *The German Ideology* still has much in common with that of the *Paris Manuscripts*. The latter redefined human nature and reinterpreted the Hegelian dialectic in terms of the metabolic interaction of man and nature in the labour-process; the technical and social determinants of this interaction are in no sense clearly distinguished. It was quite natural that Marx, in breaking with Hegel and Feuerbach, and seeking to formulate a new science of history starting from the concept of social production, should continue to conflate what he later called the forces and relations of production. The fact that it is the concept of the forces of production that is more fully developed in *The German Ideology* than the highly ambiguous 'forms of intercourse' lent itself to technological determinism as it is found in Marx's 1859 Preface to *A Contribution to the Critique of Political Economy*, where the forces of production generate changes in the relations of production. (The Preface is, to a large extent, a summary of *The German Ideology*, which remained unpublished in Marx's lifetime.) The first version of historical materialism bears some resemblance to the views of the eighteenth-century Scottish historical school, which explained historical development by changes in the 'mode of subsistence', identified mainly with the technological organization of production.[33] In *Capital*, however, the forces of production are subordinated to the relations of production: thus, the transformation of the labour-process involved in the introduction of mass factory production is attributed to the prior 'formal subsumption of labour under capital', that is, to the dominance of capitalist relations of production. (*C* i. Parts 3 and 4; for more on technological determinism, see Chapter 4 below.)

The introduction of the concept of relations of production set exploitation, social conflict, and struggle at the centre of Marx's account of historical development. It thus provided the theoretical foundation of the opening words of the *Communist Manifesto*: 'the history of hitherto existing society is the history of class struggles.' (*CW* 6:482.) It further underlay Marx's and Engels's political strategy, which saw communism as the result of the class struggle, the battle between worker and capitalist in the process of production leading to the conquest of power by the proletariat, as the prelude to the abolition of classes altogether and the creation of a society based on the co-operation of the associated producers. (See *SC* 64.) Finally, the concept of relations of production was essential to the completion of Marx's break with Hegel. Already in Hegel, history is what Althusser called 'a process without a subject', operating independently of the consciousness and will of individual actors. However, their self-seeking activities, through the 'Ruse of Reason' accomplish a purpose of which they are unaware, the self-realization of the Absolute. In this sense, history still has a subject for Hegel, but it is a peculiar one, consisting in the teleological structure of the process, which revolves back upon itself, restoring at its conclusion the original unity of Being as the self-consciousness of Absolute Spirit. For Marx, however, history has no end, no predetermined goal; it is intelligible not because it subserves the self-realization of the Absolute, or of man, but only in terms of class antagonisms generated by the relations of production. The outcome of the class struggle is not predetermined; instead of achieving social progress it may result in 'the common ruination of the contending classes' (*CW* 6:482). With the introduction of the concept of relations of production Marx finally abandons the teleological philosophy of history he inherited from Hegel and Feuerbach.[34]

If this is so, how are we to account for the presence of Hegelian categories in Marx's mature economic writings such as the *Grundrisse* and *Capital*? Are they merely, as Althusser suggests, 'survivals . . . of the influence of Hegel's thought'?[35] Or are they, as many other commentators have urged, symptoms of the basic unity of Marx's thought, from the Paris *Manuscripts* to *Capital*?[36] Often this is treated as the question of whether or not Marx uses the concepts 'human nature' and 'alienation' in his later writings. There is no doubt that he does, but, as I have already suggested, their role is very different from that in the *Manuscripts*. There the concept of human nature is used to explain historical development: indeed, history is only intelligible as the self-realization of man. On the other hand, in *Capital* Marx's theory of human nature plays no directly explanatory role; rather, it is the concept of the capitalist mode of production, and those other concepts introduced to specify its meaning, such as use-value/exchange-value, labour-process/valorization-process, constant capital/variable capital, and absolute surplus value/relative surplus value, which assume the burden of accounting for the nature and functioning of capitalist social formations. The theory of man as producer functions as a metaphysical theory, providing a philosophical rationale for some of Marx's assumptions. For example, there can be no doubt that it partially motivated Marx's choice of social labour, rather than utility (the marginal economists' preference), as the homogeneous factor underlying the variety of commodities placed on the market. However, the *truth* of the labour theory of value cannot be derived from the truth of Marx's theory of human nature, since the latter is treated as a metaphysical theory which can be neither confirmed nor refuted by experience; rather, it depends upon the falsifiable empirical hypotheses derived from it. (We shall return to the question of proof in *Capital* below.) Similarly, while numerous passages in the *Grundrisse* and *Capital* advert to the way in which capitalism, by separating the direct producer from the means of production, transposes man's productive powers onto an alien entity, capital, the concept of estranged labour is used in Marx's later writings to describe the *effects* of this mode of production rather than to account for them. As Allen W. Wood puts it, 'Marx's use of it ['alienation'] in these writings, I suggest, is no longer explanatory; rather it is descriptive or diagnostic. Marx uses the notion of alienation to identify or characterize a certain sort of human ill or dysfunction which is especially prevalent in modern society.'[37]

The key to Marx's alleged later Hegelianism is to be found in these perceptive remarks of Karl Löwith:

> How well-schooled he is in Hegel is shown less by his early writings referring directly to Hegel, which were influenced by Feuerbach, than by *Das Kapital*. The analyses in this work, although far removed from Hegel in content, are unthinkable without the incorporation of Hegel's manner of reducing a phenomenon to a notion.[38]

In other words, Hegel's influence on Marx in *Capital* consists less in any of the concepts used in that work, than in similarities in the way in which Hegel and Marx approach the problem of grasping empirical reality conceptually. If true, this claim points to a significant shift in Marx's views, since in his early writings he had forcefully attacked the 'mystery of speculative construction', as he put it in *The Holy Family*, the manner in which Hegel's dialectical method reduces empirical objects to mere semblances of genuine existence, incarnations of the Absolute. (*CW* 4:57-61.)

Lucio Colletti, under the influence of Galvano Della Volpe's interpretation of these early writings, has argued that Marx's materialism is incompatible with the Hegelian doctrine that there are contradictions in reality.[39] This claim is based on the fact that for Hegel, as we saw in Chapter 1, the discovery of contradictions in the material world reveals its insubstantiality, demonstrating that it is intelligible, not in its own terms, but as a manifestation of the Absolute. In a sense, Colletti is undoubtedly right. Attempts to construct a Marxist 'dialectical' logic in place of 'bourgeois' formal logic follow Hegel in repudiating the law of non-contradiction. This principle forbids the assertion of a proposition and its negation. (Formally, the principle is '-(p.-p)'.) The sentence 'It is raining and it is not raining', for example, violates the law of non-contradiction. From such a sentence all other sentences may be validly inferred. Therefore, to assert a contradiction is to say *everything*. It is also to say nothing, for any definite statement rules out the existence of certain states of affairs. (To say 'It's raining' is to deny that it is not raining.) Rejection of the law of non-contradiction would make discourse impossible.[40] Hegel's claim that this principle would make movement and change inexplicable is entirely spurious, and derives largely from the temporary impasse in which the calculus found itself at the beginning of the nineteenth century.[41]

There is nothing in any of Marx's writings to justify burdening him with the absurd doctrine that the law of non-contradiction is invalid. It does not follow, however, that the concept of 'real contradictions' is absent from *Capital*. On the contrary, Marx is highly critical of those who seek to eliminate contradictions from reality. For example, he wrote of James Mill:

> Where the economic relation – and therefore also the categories expressing it – includes contradictions, opposites, and likewise the unity of opposites, he emphasises the aspect of the *unity* of the contradictions and denies the contradictions. He transforms the unity of opposites into the direct identity of opposites. (*TSV* iii. 87-8.)

Elsewhere he wrote that the capitalist accumulation process involves 'a contradiction which manifests itself in contradictory tendencies and phenomena. . . . Crises are always but momentary and forcible solutions of the existing contradictions.' (*C* iii. 249; see also *TSV* ii. 500.)

These passages give us some idea of the role played by contradictions in *Capital*. Hegel had attacked the reflective understanding's 'tenderness for *things*, whose only care is that they shall not contradict one another' (*GL* ii. 50), because he wished to show that the reality of the material world lay not in its self-subsistence but derived rather from its role as the self-estranged form of the Absolute. Marx attacked those who denied the existence of contradictions in reality because of their tenderness for *capitalist society*. For Marx the statement that reality is contradictory means that class struggle, social conflict, and economic crises are not epiphenomena, not the products of accident, merely incidental to the working of society, but are *endemic* to every social formation divided into classes, revealing its historically specific, and temporary nature. Contradiction is the moving principle of social life. Social formations will submit to scientific knowledge only if conceptualized in terms of the antagonistic relations of production constituting them: the dialectic,

> in its rational form . . . is a scandal and an abomination to the bourgeoisie and its doctrinaire spokesmen, because it includes in its positive understanding of what exists a simultaneous recognition of its negation, of its inevitable destruction; because it regards every historically developed form as being in a fluid state, in motion, and therefore grasps its transient aspect as well; and because it does not let itself be impressed by anything, being in its very essence critical and revolutionary. (*C* i. 103.)

Thus understood, the Marxian dialectic involves neither the denial of the principle of non-contradiction, nor acceptance of the suspect notion, which we shall touch on in Chapter 3, of a dialectic of nature. The latter concept provides the corner-stone of 'dialectical materialism' in the form in which it is found in the Soviet Union and its client-states. Contradiction is held by this doctrine to be an essential property of nature as well as of society. The effect is to transform Marxism into an ontology, a general account of the fundamental structure of reality. There are at least three difficulties with such an approach. First, it is vulnerable to the criticisms of the Hegelian dialectic by Adorno, Althusser, and Della Volpe as a theodicy which resumes the heterogeneity characteristic of reality into the unity of Being. Secondly, and more specifically, the effect of seeking to justify historical materialism as a scientific research programme in terms of a more general metaphysical theory is to render it immune to empirical falsification. Thirdly, it is difficult to give much content to the claim that this or that development in, say, subatomic physics or molecular biology instantiates, or proves the truth of the laws of the dialectic. It would seem far preferable to restrict the extension of the concept of contradiction to the analysis of social formations. Marx's own usage suggests that we should use the concept to denote not so much social conflict as such antagonisms as are constitutive of a mode of production, and which are therefore inherent in its structure independent of their empirical manifestation. An example would be the antagonisms between capital and labour, and between individual units of capital, characteristic of the capitalist mode of production. This case brings out a further property of contradiction – that the terms of a contradictory relation are themselves constituted by that relation. Thus, as Marx frequently emphasizes, capital and wage-labour are inseparable; similarly, it is the process of competition between capitals that compels them to behave as capitals.[42]

Marx's later Hegelianism is primarily methodological.[43] *Capital* places great emphasis on the contrast between the underlying internal structure of the capitalist mode of production and its surface appearance. Different economic schools are judged by the degree to which they succeed in penetrating beneath the surface. It is on this basis that Marx distinguishes between 'classical political economy, . . . all the economists who . . . have investigated the real internal framework of bourgeois relations of production', and the 'vulgar economists who flounder around within the apparent framework of those relations' (*C* i. 174-5, n. 34). Ricardo's greatness lies in the fact that his starting point is an abstraction, the labour theory of value, even though it contradicts the apparent movement of empirically given relative prices. 'At last Ricardo steps in and calls to science: Halt! The basis, the starting-point for the physiology of the bourgeois system – for the understanding of its internal organic coherence and life-process – is the determination of *value by labour-time*.' (*TSV* ii. 165-6) Marx describes his own method as that of 'rising from the abstract to the concrete' (*G* 101), of explaining the observable movement of the economy starting from the socially necessary labour-time involved in the production of commodities. However, he seeks to avoid what he regards as Ricardo's errors. These spring, Marx argues, from Ricardo's taking as one of his axioms the empirical fact that returns on capital in different sectors are equalized (i.e. that a general rate of profit exists). But, Ricardo himself shows that if conditions of production are not uniform, and if a general rate of profit exists, then commodities will not exchange at their values, i.e. the socially necessary labour-time required to produce them. So two of Ricardo's basic postulates – the labour theory of value and the assumption of equal returns on capital – are mutually incompatible.

Ricardo was aware of this anomaly, but treated it as introducing only minor quantitative discrepancies into his system – commodities would still fluctuate broadly around their values. But the contradiction encouraged his successors gradually to abandon the labour theory of value. Marx argued that the problem arose from a methodological error on Ricardo's part:

> Instead of *postulating* this *general rate of profit*, Ricardo should rather have examined in how far its *existence* is in fact consistent with the determination of value by labour-time, and he would have found that instead of being consistent with it, prima facie, it *contradicts* it, and that its existence would therefore have to be explained through a number of intermediary stages, a procedure which is very different from merely including it under the law of value. (TSV ii. 174.)

And in *Capital* Marx proceeds precisely in this way, trying to explain those empirically observable pheonomena which appear to refute the labour theory of value 'through a number of intermediary stages'. Having analysed 'capital-in-general', the process of production, and the process of circulation, in Volumes i and ii respectively, in Volume iii Marx considers the process of competition between 'many capitals'. He shows that competition will lead to the formation of a general rate of profit and that in these circumstances commodities will exchange, not at their values (the socially necessary labour-time involved in their production), but rather at their modified values, or prices of production, formed through the redistribution of surplus-value among capitals in proportion to the extent to which their individual rates of profit are above or below the average. Thus the validity of the labour theory of value is inseparable from that of the entire system of propositions constituting *Capital*. 'Science',

Marx wrote in response to criticisms that he had failed to prove the theory at the beginning of Volume i, 'consists precisely in demonstrating *how* the law of value asserts itself. So that if one wanted at the very beginning to "explain" all the phenomena which seemingly contradict that law, one would have to present the science *before* science' (*SC* 196).

This conception of scientific method is deeply influenced by Hegel, who criticized Kant's concept of judgement because it involved an abstract conception of universality. For Kant, universal concepts are distinct from their particular instances; judgement proceeds by subsumption, merely including these instances under some general concept without establishing any internal connection between the two. Abstraction, Hegel argued, 'omits the particular, and ascends to higher and highest genus' (*GL* ii. 257), creating a hierarchical deductive system which classifies, but does not explain, the empirical material included under it. To this Hegel counterposed the concrete universal, 'no mere sum of features common to several things, confronted by a particular which enjoys an existence of its own' but rather 'self-particularizing or self-specifying' (*LL* 227). The concrete universal is inseparably united with its particular instances, forming together with them an organic whole. This conception of the universal as a synthesis of particulars is closely connected with Hegel's critique of the concept of scientific proof as it had been accepted since Aristotle's *Posterior Analytics*. On the traditional conception, each science forms a deductive system derived from certain axioms, whose truth is either self-evident, or arrived at by induction from observation. Truth is transferred downwards in the system, from the axioms to the propositions that may be inferred from them; empirical material is explained by being classified within this system. Everything turns on the proof of the original axioms, as Hegel puts it, 'as though the proposition were before us here, and the proof were something separate from it'. But for Hegel 'the proof comes with the proposition': the truth of the propositions composing his system is established only in the course of the development of that system.[44]

The parallels with Marx's approach in *Capital* are very clear. Marx's criticism of Ricardo is precisely that the latter treats value as an abstract universal, from which descriptions of the empirical phenomena may be directly derived. Thus, Ricardo's method involves 'formal abstraction', 'regarding the phenomenal form as *immediate and direct* proof or exposition of the general laws, and . . . failing to *interpret* it' (TSV ii. 106). By contrast, Marx's own approach of 'rising from the abstract to the concrete', involves proceeding by 'intermediary stages', and showing in the process how a variety of empirical phenomena which apparently contradict the labour theory of value can only be explained starting from it. 'Science consists precisely in demonstrating *how* the law of value asserts itself'; as in Hegel, 'the proof comes with the proposition', being inseparable from the ensemble of propositions forming *Capital*. The result is 'a totality of thoughts, concrete in thought'; as such, 'the concrete is concrete because it is the concentration of many determinations, hence unity of the diverse' (G101). In other words, value for Marx is a *concrete universal*, forming an organic whole with the empirical phenomena which it explains.

Do these parallels demonstrate an identity of method in Hegel's *Logic* and Marx's *Capital*? The answer to this question must be a negative one. As Marx himself had shown in his *Critique of Hegel's Philosophy of Right*, Hegel's dialectical method reduces the empirical material it purports to explain into mere exemplifications of the Idea. It is easy to account for this discrepancy between what Hegel purports to do and what he actually does. As we saw in Chapter 1, the dialectical method is identical to the Absolute Idea, or, to put it another way, the latter is nothing else but the process of attaining itself, whose structure is that of a dialectical triad, original unity, self-estrangement, and reconciliation in a higher unity. Now while this structure 'explains' specific phenomena, weaving them into a wider pattern, it does so teleologically, so that their meaning consists in nothing other than their contribution to the goal of the process, the Absolute Idea's achievement of full self-consciousness. Necessarily, therefore, the empirical material included in Hegel's system is evaporated, reduced to mere illustrations of Spirit's progress through the world. Hegel's system is a closed one: 'contradiction is not the end of the matter,' he writes, 'but cancels itself.' (LL 174.) Its role is to give Being a concrete content and then, in the negation of negation, to resume that content back into the Absolute. For Marx, however, history is an open process, and contradiction is constitutive of social reality, providing the motor of historical change (in the shape of the conflict between the forces and relations of production) even under communism. He could not, therefore, simply take over Hegel's method, for it is inseparable from his system, and can explain phenomena only by dissolving them into a teleological structure.

Marx's reliance on Hegel's methodological guidance was, therefore, a hazardous enterprise, as is shown by those cases where he took seriously his own injunction to invert Hegel and set the dialectic on its feet (*C* i. 103). For example, in the *Grundrisse* capital tends to take on the properties of the Absolute Idea, and to 'posit' its 'presuppositions', i.e. to generate its own conditions of existence, in a manner suspiciously similar to the way in which the logical categories produce their own content, and the the way in which Idea produces nature (e.g. *G* 459 ff.). The same is not true of *Capital*, where, with certain exceptions (see, for example, Chapter 6 Section 1 below on the theory of fetishism), the use of Hegelian categories and motifs is almost wholly subordinated to the empirical task of investigating capitalism. The structure of *Capital* is radically anti-Hegelian: it culminates, not in the reconciliation of contradictions in a higher unity, but in 'the *class struggle*, into which the movement and the smash-up of the whole business resolves itself' (*SC* 195). Later Marxists were not, however, so fortunate in avoiding the difficulties involved in a materialist appropriation of Hegel.

3. The Return of the Repressed

(1) The Marxisms of the Second International

Marx's 'return to Hegel' in his mature economic writings was a surreptitious one. It was left to others to attempt to construct a specifically Marxist philosophical tradition. Forty years after the founders of historical materialism had 'settled accounts' with their 'erstwhile philosophical conscience',[1] Engels laid claim to classical idealism: 'the German working-class movement is the inheritor of German classical philosophy.' (SW iii. 376.) Engels's philosophical intervention was part of his enormous contribution to the theoretical and political formation of the German Social Democratic party (SPD), created by the fusion of the Marxist and Lassallean socialists in 1875.[2] His main philosophical works, Anti-Dühring (1878), 'Ludwig Feuerbach and the End of Classical German Philosophy' (1886), and the posthumously published Dialectics of Nature (1925), were largely intended to wrest the fledgling party from alien ideological influences, and in particular from that of ethical socialism, stemming from the 'true socialists', whose concoctions of Fichtean idealism and Feuerbachian humanism Marx and Engels had already attacked in the 1840s.[3] Engels sought to do this by presenting the picture of a universe governed by certain objective, generally applicable, scientifically ascertainable laws. Historical materialism, he argued, had discovered the specific version of these laws operative in the realm of human society. Knowledge of these laws is essential to the success of a socialist party, since the proletarian revolution will be the outcome of an objective social process. Socialism must be scientific, conceptualizing the material conditions of change, and not Utopian, concerned merely with the critique of existing society and the depiction of a future one. Hegel's importance lies in his revolutionary dialectical method imprisoned within a conservative idealist system: 'dialectics is conceived as the science of the most general laws of *all* motion. This implies that its laws must be valid just as much for motion in nature and human

61

history as for the motion of thought.'[4] These laws, extracted by Engels from Hegel's *Logic*, were three in number, the transformation of quantity into quality, and vice versa, the interpenetration of opposites, and the negation of the negation. They were instantiated, Engels believed, by all the major scientific discoveries of the nineteenth century – by Darwin's *Origin of Species* as well as Marx's *Capital*.

It should be clear from the two preceding chapters that such an attempt to rescue the formal structure of Hegel's dialectic while rejecting his idealism is doomed to failure, since the method itself is identical to the Absolute Idea: in particular, it is through the negation of the negation that the difference constitutive of the material world is resumed into the identity of the Notion. Furthermore, the concept of a dialectic of nature, when taken seriously as providing criteria for the construction of scientific hypotheses, has interfered with genuine research and encouraged pseudo-scientific drivel, most notoriously in the Lysenko affair.[5] It has been common, especially among Marxists of a humanist persuasion, to blame all this on Engels. There is no doubt that Marx was generally more cautious than Engels in the claims he made for historical materialism, for example, criticizing the Russian populist writer N. K. Mikhailovsky for 'transforming my historical sketch of the genesis of capitalism in western Europe [Part 8 of *Capital*, volume i] into a historico-philosophic theory of the general path of development prescribed by fate to all nations, whatever the circumstances in which they find themselves' (*SC* 293). There is no evidence, however, that Marx rejected Engels's rehabilitation of the Hegelian dialectic. Indeed, he contributed one chapter to *Anti-Dühring* (which was published five years before his death in 1883) and in *Capital* cited the molecular theory of chemistry as an instance of 'the law discovered by Hegel, in his *Logic*, that at a certain point merely quantitative distinctions pass over by a dialectical inversion into qualitative distinctions' (*C* i. 423).

In any case, what has come to be known as dialectical materialism became the official ideology of German social democracy and, given the SPD's enormous weight in the second International (1889-1914), of much of the European working-class movement. In the hands of the second International's chief theoreticians, Karl Kautsky, Georgi Plekhanov, and Antonio Labriola, the dialectic, conceived as an ontology, an account of the fundamental nature of being, served to justify a version of Marxism in which social change is an organic process whose outcome is determined in advance. 'The capitalist social system has run its course,' Kautsky wrote in 1892; 'its dissolution is now only a question of time. Irresistible economic forces lead with the certainty of doom to the shipwreck of capitalist production. The substitution of a new social order for the existing one is no longer desirable, it has become inevitable.'[6]

Such an evolutionist version of Marxism could claim support from Chapter 32 of *Capital*, Volume i, 'The Historical Tendency of Capitalist Accumulation', where Marx discovered a Hegelian triad in bourgeois society's historical trajectory. The original unity was that of direct producer and means of production in pre-capitalist social formations. Then came 'the first negation of individual private property', the expropriation of the direct producer and the monopolization of the means of production by a small minority. 'But capitalist production begets, with the inexorability of a natural process, its own negation. This is the negation of the negation', in which the working class created by capitalism resumes control of the means of production (*C* i. 929-30). And indeed Plekhanov, the most philosophically erudite of the 'orthodox' Marxists of the second International, derived precisely such a historical teleology, in which the outcome of the process is predetermined, from his reading of Hegel. '*The irresistible striving to the great historical goal*,' he wrote in 'On the Sixtieth Anniversary of Hegel's Death' (1891), '*a striving which nothing can stop — such is the legacy of the great German idealist philosophy*.'[7]

There were, moreover, other influences, for example, the vulgarizations of Darwin's theory of evolution by Ernst Haeckel and others. Massimo Salvadori writes in his major study of Kautsky:

In 1924, recalling the period of his own formation, Kautsky was to say that when Darwinism 'conquered the ranks of culture', he also had accepted it 'with enthusiasm' and that his 'theory of history was intended to be nothing other than the application of Darwinism to social development'. This fusion of Marxism and Darwinism served to inspire Kautsky with a conception of the revolutionary process as the development of an organic necessity. There was not room for illusions that anything which had been historically condemned by evolution could be conserved or that anyone could voluntaristically force the pace of evolution itself.[8]

Underlying Marxism's evolutionist turn was a complex social process. The SPD and its allied trade unions were mass organizations enjoying the support of millions of workers and they were intransigently opposed to a regime which had, during the years of the Anti-Socialist Laws (1878-90), sought virtually to suppress them. At the same time, there evolved within the party and the unions a full-time apparatus whose raison d'être was increasingly that of the negotiation of compromise and the avoidance of conflict, and whose concern tended to be that of preserving the movement intact at the price of avoiding class struggle.[9] Gramsci and Benjamin have both suggested that the belief in the inevitability of socialism played an important ideological role in the second International, the certainty of future victory giving party and union militants an incentive to remain active, however bleak the immediate situation; it also served to justify the abstention from any activity which might provoke a direct confrontation between the workers' movement and the State.[10]

The delicate balance struck by German social democracy was evident as early as 1891, when the Erfurt Programme was adopted. This document, criticized at the time by Engels for its failure to admit the necessity of forcibly overthrowing Prussian absolutism (SW iii. 433 ff.), was divided into two parts. The first, or maximum programme, by Kautsky, surveyed the contradictions of capitalism and announced its inevitable collapse. Eduard Bernstein, in the second part, set out the SPD's minimum programme, its immediate demands, especially for the democratization of the German state. History would close the gap between maximum and minimum programmes, bringing about proletarian revolution by 'natural necessity' (a favourite phrase of Kautsky's). This would take place through the election of a socialist majority to the Reichstag, as the culmination of the parliamentary tactics through which the SPD sought to implement its minimum programme. Any attempt to speed up the historical process by extra-parliamentary mass action would, Kautsky argued in 1910 and 1912, when defending the SPD's strategy of attrition (Ermattungsstrategie) against Rosa Luxemburg and Anton Pannekoek, only endanger the gains already made by the workers' movement.[11]

The vulgarized, evolutionist version of Hegel's dialectic characteristic of the 'orthodox' Marxism of the second International thus served to provide both a guarantee of the success of the socialist revolution and a justification of the essentially reformist and gradualist strategy pursued by the SPD and other European workers' parties. It was, therefore, natural that the challenges to this orthodoxy should be both philosophical and political. The first of many 'crises of Marxism' can be dated from the appearance in 1899 of Bernstein's *Die Voraussetzungen des Sozialismus und die Aufgaben der Sozialdemokratie*. This attack on 'orthodox' Marxism amounted theoretically to little more than a reversion to 'true' socialism, rejecting as it did the dialectic, historical materialism, the labour theory of value, and indeed the bulk of *Capital*, and advocating the reinstatement of Kantian ethics. Politically, however, the book was dynamite. Bernstein called on the SPD to bring its theory into line with its practice, demanding that German social democracy should 'make up its mind to appear what it is in reality: a democratic, socialistic party of reform'.[12] The embarrassed party leadership secured Bernstein's formal condemnation for theoretical 'revisionism', but permitted the increasingly vocal right wing for which he was the spokesman to remain within the SPD. Kautsky admitted in a letter to August Bebel that 'if Bernstein had written his *Voraussetzungen* when Engels was still alive, the General would not have treated him as delicately as we have, but would have dispatched him with a kick and a cry of "Out, scoundrel!"'[13] For Bebel and Kautsky, Bernstein's crime was to have blurted out what was better left unsaid. 'My dear Ede,' Ignaz Auer, the SPD secretary, protested to Bernstein, 'one doesn't *say* such things, one simply *does* them.'[14]

The cat was out of the bag: the 'Bernsteiniad' marked the beginning of a debate within German and then European socialism which was to continue with growing bitterness until after the First World War, by which time the second International had split into three. This division was prefigured in the SPD, which by 1910 had three wings: right, left, and centre. Left and right agreed on little except the need to revise the 'party tactic', which Kautsky and the centre continued to defend. The right, with considerable support from the trade union leadership, increasingly influential within SPD counsels after 1905, wanted to scrap the maximum programme, drop the party's stance of principled opposition to the Wilhemine monarchy, and support the German state in its conflicts with the other great powers: August 1914 marked their triumph. The left, and above all Rosa Luxemburg in her 1910 polemic with Kautsky, proposed that the SPD encourage mass strikes in order to force through the party's minimum democratic programme and build up the working-class consciousness and organization necessary to conquer political power. The centre, formally critical of the right, gravitated towards them. The debate would culminate after the German revolution of 1918 in right-wing SPD ministers presiding over the murder of Luxemburg and Karl Liebknecht.

It is of great interest to note the way in which the different political positions, as they emerged between 1900 and 1914, often involved a theoretical critique of the evolutionist Marxism of Kautsky and Plekhanov. Thus, on the one hand, the theoreticians of Austrian social democracy (the SPÖ), the Austro-Marxists, sought to give orthodoxy firmer, neo-Kantian foundations, while Lenin, Trotsky and Luxemburg subverted orthodoxy from within.

Politically, Austro-Marxism was closest to the Kautskyite centre: even after the European workers' movement had split into the second and third Internationals, Otto Bauer and the other leaders of Austrian social democracy sought to reconcile revolution and reform, left and right. At the same time, the SPÖ eschewed armed confrontation with the State, a policy which led to the destruction of the Austrian workers' movement by the Dolfuss regime in February 1934.[15] The Austro-Marxists sympathized with Bernstein theoretically to the extent that, like him, they believed ethics to be autonomous of classes: thus Rudolph Hilferding argued that one can logically accept the truth of Marxism as a scientific theory yet reject socialism as an ethical and political stance.[16] But their primary philosophical interest was to provide historical materialism as a science with adequate philosophical foundations. Under the influence of both neo-Kantianism (see Section 2 below), and the empirio-monism of Ernst Mach, they believed that Kautsky's evolutionism had failed to do so, having played the role chiefly of a popularization of Marxism that was also, inevitably, a vulgarization. Max Adler, the main Austro-Marxist philosopher, 'accepted neo-Kantianism', according to Bauer, 'in order to defend the Marxist science of society against all revisionist dilution with the help of the Kantian critique of knowledge, and to distinguish it sharply from the ethical justification of socialism'.[17]

The interest of Adler's work lies in the fact that it was the first major attempt to reintroduce the corner-stone of German classical idealism, the transcendental subject, into Marxism. Indeed, his 'transcendental deduction' of historical materialism from the presuppositions of consciousness strikingly anticipates what is sometimes described as Wittgenstein's essentially Kantian attempt to prove that our ability even to describe our sensations depends on the existence of public discourse and social 'forms of life'.[18] 'The critical philosophy', Adler argued, 'starts, and must start, from individual consciousness, but demonstrates in this consciousness a supra-individual, transcendental-social, a priori, socialized character.'[19] Kant thereby established the basic concept of historical materialism, sociation (Vergesellschaftung), according to which, Adler asserted in a critical discussion of Max Weber, 'all "understanding" in the psychological sense presupposes a definite constitution of the individual consciousness in which the immanent interrelatedness of self-consciousness depends on the consciousness of others'[20] – in other words, the individual 'I' presupposes the social 'We'. It is this transcendental condition of experience which permits Marxism to discover causal regularities in social life, just as the transcendental deduction of the categories gives scientists' establishment of natural-scientific laws a rational basis. This argument involves a certain subjectivization of Marxism: 'the materialist conception of history and the theory of social progress', Adler writes, 'derive their meaning and their certainty from the concept of socialized man, or ... socialized consciousness.'[21] It is interesting, therefore, to note a tendency on the part of Austro-Marxists to identify social relations with forms of consciousness, and to accord great significance to ideological, as opposed to economic and political struggles.[22] In these respects, they were precursors of Western Marxism.

Meanwhile, on the revolutionary left wing of the second International, Lenin, Luxemburg, and Trotsky developed analyses of specific questions which represented a philosophical as well as political break with the evolutionism of Kautsky and Plekhanov. These analyses involved a shift towards a version of Marxism which laid much greater stress on the role of consciousness and activity in the revoutionary process. That they amounted to a break with, and not merely a permutation of, 'orthodox' Marxism was not consciously formulated by the authors of these theories. Indeed, Lenin and Trotsky continued to have the greatest respect for Kautsky right up to the catastrophe of August 1914, and supported him in the 1910 polemic with Luxemburg over the 'party tactic'.[23] Yet Lenin, in particular, even though he regarded himself as a loyal follower of Kautsky, developed in his approach to the specific problems of building a revolutionary workers' party in Tsarist Russia a radically non-evolutionist version of Marxism.[24]

Orthodoxy conceived history as a series of modes of production succeeding each other in a pre-ordained sequence in response to the level of development of the productive forces. The class struggle acted merely as the executor of the laws of history. Backward countries such as Russia were fated to pass through a capitalist stage of development: only thus would the material preconditions of socialism be created. Moreover, once established, capitalism would beget its overthrow 'with the inexorability of a natural process'. This belief in the inevitability of socialism was shared even by Marx and Engels, though they rejected the notion of an inevitable economic breakdown of capitalism. Capitalism, by bringing together large numbers of workers in single units of production, provided the material basis on which class consciousness could develop. Experience of their common exploitation would lead workers to band together against the employers and in defence of their economic interests. From these elemental class battles, and the organisations they threw up, would develop a united proletariat which, as a revolutionary 'class-for-itself', would seek the overthrow of the capitalist system. 'The great thing', Engels wrote in 1886, 'is to get the working class to move *as a class*; that once obtained, they will soon find the right direction.' (*SC* 376.)[25]

Lenin's 'practical break' (as Althusser would put it) with evolutionism involved three propositions. First, class struggles do not have an inevitable outcome. There are always *alternative paths* of historical development. Second, the contradictions which load history in a particular direction are not purely economic: they depend, that is, not only on the relations and forces of production but on the political and ideological relations with which they are bound up. Third, the conditions of social revolution will not arise automatically, as a result of the expansion of the productive forces, but require the active, conscious, and organized intervention of revolutionaries. Two examples will illustrate these propositions at work in Lenin's thought. Lenin agreed with orthodoxy (in this case embodied by Plekhanov) to the extent of believing that the overthrow of Tsarism would be a bourgeois revolution, confining itself to creating a framework within which capitalism can freely develop. However, he stressed that there were different paths to capitalist development. The one Russia was already following involved an alliance between industrial capitalists and feudal landowners: its most likely outcome would be a quasi-absolutist state along the lines of Wilhemine Germany. The other, involving the revolutionary overthrow of Tsarism and the destruction of the great estates by an alliance of workers and peasants, would sweep away the remnants of feudalism and permit the rapid development of capitalism. Rather than remain neutral between these different types of bourgeois revolution, the proletariat should do its utmost to ensure that Russia took the second path, which would permit a rapid transition to socialism. This would involve the working class playing the leading role in the revolutionary process, since the liberal bourgeoisie was already heavily dependent on the regime and on Western capital. Against Plekhanov and the Mensheviks, who believed that Russian social democracy should confine itself to giving critical support to the liberals and let history take its inevitable course, Lenin quoted the eleventh thesis on Feuerbach, and accused them of 'ignoring the active, leading, and guiding part which can and must be played in history by parties which have realized the material prerequisites of a revolution and have placed themselves at the head of the progressive classes'.[26]

Closely connected to this argument was Lenin's denial, in *What is to be Done?* (1902), that 'the working class *spontaneously* gravitates towards socialism'.[27] The belief that revolutionary consciousness would not arise inevitably from the pressure of economic circumstances, but would depend instead on the intervention of a Marxist party, provided the corner-stone of Lenin's views on organization. Indeed, Lenin's most important theoretical achievement was to make organization an important issue within Marxism; both Luxemburg and Trotsky tended to see the formation of class consciousness as an organic process, with revolution as the inevitable result of the working class's experience of class struggle. Only Lenin grasped that organizational questions, and above all the existence of an experienced revolutionary party deeply implanted in the proletariat, would be decisive in the struggle for power: the experience of the Russian and German revolutions was to prove him right.

There were, of course, important *lacunae* in Lenin's thought. *What is to be Done?* tends to ignore the manner in which mass struggles serve as a means of self-education for the working class; it was left to Luxemburg to recall the stress of the 'Theses on Feuerbach' upon the role of involvement in social practice in the transformation of consciousness. It was only after the revolution of 1905 that Lenin came to stress that revolutionary consciousness results from an *interaction* between the masses, themselves conditioned by their material circumstances, and the Party: he wrote in 1907 that 'the working class . . . for objective economic reasons possesses a greater capacity for organization than any other class of capitalist society. Without this condition an organization of professional revolutionaries would be nothing more than a plaything, an adventure, a mere signboard.'[28] Again it was Trotsky who argued that the Russian proletariat, once it had overthrown Tsarism, would be unable to remain within the bounds of capitalism and would be forced to take power for itself and to introduce socialist measures. Whether such a regime would survive would depend on whether the revolution spread to the advanced capitalist countries; even if the material conditions of socialism did not exist in Russia, they were present on a world scale, thanks to the creation by capitalism of an international economy. This theory of permanent revolution, adopted by Lenin on his return to Russia in April 1917, was to be confirmed by the October revolution, and by the subsequent fate of the state it created.

(2) Lukács and Hegelian Marxism

The political and theoretical rupture of revolutionary from 'orthodox' Marxism was only brought to fruition in August 1914, when the bulk of the second International decided to support the war. The most important impulse behind the great efflorescence of Marxist philosophy at the end of the First World War was the belief that the October Revolution and the breakup of the second International required a reformulation of the basic principles of historical materialism. The Bolsheviks represented the triumph of consciousness, action, and organization over the iron laws of history, such was the lesson drawn by the young Gramsci in his famous article welcoming the October uprising, 'The Revolution against *Capital*'.[29] It was the context of an attempt to translate the lessons of October into a new, non-evolutionist Marxism that there occurred the great 'return to Hegel' with which the names of Georg Lukács, Antonio Gramsci, and Karl Korsch are associated.

The most important philosophical influence on these thinkers was in fact less Hegel (although I shall continue to call them the 'Hegelian Marxists' for convenience's sake) than the anti-naturalist revolt at the turn of the nineteenth century. This movement had its greatest dimensions in Germany, where it developed in reaction to the mid-century scientific materialism of Moleschott, Büchner, Gruppe, and others, and embraced a variety of currents of thought – the two main neo-Kantian schools at Marburg and Heidelberg, as well as Dilthey, Weber, Frege, and Husserl. But it had important counterparts elsewhere – Bergson in France, Croce in Italy, Bradley in England.

While the general (although not universal) tendency of these philosophers was idealist, reasserting the primacy of the subject over the material world, common to all was a rejection of naturalism, in the sense of the belief that the methods of the natural sciences can be extended to the study of man. (See also Chapter 4 below.) We have seen how such a belief was involved in the Enlightenment's attempt to set the moral sciences on a firm, empirical basis. By the mid-nineteenth century this had come to mean a reductive physicalism which denied reality to anything but matter and motion.[30] Basic to the revolt against naturalism was the denial that social and cultural phenomena can be explained by the sort of universal causal laws characteristic of the physical sciences. Instead, in a variety of forms – Dilthey's concept of hermeneutic understanding, Windelband's distinction between ideographic and nomothetic sciences, Croce's dismissal of the natural sciences as composed of pseudo-concepts which abstracted from specific spatio-temporal contexts, Bergson's counterposition of *durée*, an organic, irreversible, swelling out of the past into the future, to the physicist's repetition of instantaneous presents – the anti-naturalists insisted that social and cultural phenomena were unique, historically specific experiences unamenable to inclusion in the abstract deductive systems constructed by the natural scientists. Equally, the transcendental subject was reinstated to play the role of constituting social experience. In the social and cultural world, anti-naturalists tended to argue, man confronted his own creations; here the old Hegelian model of knowledge as the identity of subject and object, hopelessly speculative when applied to nature, found its true significance. Finally, while Kant had distinguished between theoretical and practical reason, understanding and will, natural sciences and ethics, attributing cognitive status only to the first term in each of these contrasts, the anti-naturalists tended to run these two spheres together, and to give primacy to the will. They consequently treated scientific theories less as reflections of an objectively existing reality than as the free creations of the human mind, constructed with a view to their elegance, simplicity, or utility rather than to their truth. Here anti-naturalism converged with the pragmatism of James, Peirce, and Dewey, and with Duhem's and Poincaré's conventionalism, whose tendency was also to deny that the sciences could be at the same time objectively true, and derived from experience.

In essence, the Hegelian Marxism of Lukács, Korsch, and Gramsci, like the Austro-Marxism of Bauer and Adler, amounted to the reinterpretation of historical materialism along anti-naturalist lines. Kautskyianism could be legitimately regarded as the induction of naturalism into Marxism, treating history as a process governed by universal causal laws, and thus legitimating a fatalist refusal to engage in revolutionary action. But while the Austrian theorists had contented themselves with an epistem-ological reworking of 'orthodox' Marxism which left its content largely untouched, the Hegelians sought to recast Marxism conceptually and thereby to justify the revolutionary strategy of the Bolsheviks and the third International. The anti-naturalists gave primacy to an abstract mental faculty; the Hegelian Marxists set in its place *social practice*, conceived as the interaction of subject and object. They used this concept as a lens through which to view, and resolve three problems: the relation of thought and reality, and, specifically, of Marxism's epistemo-logical justification, of its right to call itself *scientific* socialism; the relation of economic base and politico-ideological superstruc-ture; and the relation of theory to practice. This conflation of three arguably distinct issues was made possible by the categories of subject and object, and by the belief that social reality was characterized by the basic identity of subject and object, or, as Korsch put it, by '*the coincidence of consciousness and reality'.*[31] The effect, when applied to the first of these questions, was a pragmatist epistemology. This can be seen most clearly in Gramsci's case. Profoundly influenced by Croce, Gramsci went as far as to deny the existence of a reality independent of human consciousness and actions. Scientific theories, he argued, have no truth-value independent of the circumstances of their formulation; they serve to articulate and render coherent the aspirations of specific classes to power.[32]

Lenin's encounter with Hegel in the *Philosophical Notebooks* is so much at odds with all this as to seem positively eccentric.[33] His first philosophical intervention, in *Materialism and Empirio-Criticism* (1908), was devoted to defending the realist thesis that thought merely reflects an independently existing reality. His reading of the *Logic* did not lead Lenin to reject this realism, but rather to place less emphasis on, or perhaps to abandon, the causal theory of perception put forward in the earlier book as an account of how thought reflects reality. In the *Notebooks* he tended rather to stress the conceptual character of knowledge, writing, for example, that 'the reflection of nature in human cognition . . . consists precisely of concepts, laws, categories, etc.'.[34] Beyond this Lenin's later views on the dialectic are of interest chiefly for the degree to which they parallel those of Marx. He stressed the pervasive and fundamental nature of contradiction: 'the unity (coincidence, identity, equal action) of opposites is conditional, temporary, relative, the struggle of mutually exclusive opposites is absolute, just as development and motion are absolute.'[35] Closely connected with this is a stress on the complexity of reality – 'there are *no* "pure" phenomena, nor can there be, either in nature or society'[36] – which served to justify its conceptual reconstruction starting from theoretical abstractions. The latter point is, of course, especially close to Marx's methodological reflections in the Introduction to the *Grundrisse*.

The philosophical interest of Lenin's writings lies, however, less in any epistemological or ontological doctrine expounded in them than in the texture of the thought they reveal, the method at work in them. Lenin displayed a capacity perhaps unequalled by any other Marxist to grasp the concrete as (in Marx's words) 'the concentration of many determinations', to recognize the unique characteristics of a specific situation without losing sight of the general theoretical principles on which his analyses were based.

If Lenin's writings are perhaps too dry to possess the succulence which Trotsky ascribed to dialectical concepts, they nevertheless display the operation of the method advocated by Marx in the *Grundrisse* of 'rising from the abstract to the concrete'. This virtue was as much political as theoretical. Lenin's dialectic combined enormous tactical flexibility with a single-minded determination to achieve the final goal, the conquest of political power and construction of communism. Kautsky and the SPD had made a fetish of a single, parliamentary tactic; Lenin was prepared to pursue a variety of different tactics in pursuit of proletarian revolution. This 'revolutionary *Realpolitik*', as Lukács aptly called it, reflected the objective position of the working class within capitalist relations of production: the creation of bourgeois society, yet impelled to challenge it, continually engaged in both the struggle *within* capitalism and the struggle *against* capitalism.[37]

The version of Marxism expounded in Lukács's *History and Class Consciousness* (1923) is, by contrast, Utopian and messianic in its conception of the proletariat as the absolute negation of bourgeois society. This book, the masterwork of Hegelian Marxism, and one of the most influential philosophical works of the twentieth century, is a systematic attempt to restate, within a Marxist framework, the anti-naturalism Lukács had already developed before becoming a revolutionary, especially during his involvement with Max Weber's Heidelberg Circle.[38] In his most important pre-Marxist text, *The Theory of the Novel* (1916), Lukács espoused what he would in retrospect call 'the philosophically as well as politically uncertain attitude of romantic anti-capitalism'.[39] Here he counterposed the harmonious, organic totality of Homeric Greece's 'integrated civilization' to the 'tragic' fissure dividing individual and community, subject and object, 'ought' and 'is' in modern times. The experience of the First World War, and the revolutionary wave which shook central and eastern Europe at its conclusion, transformed this 'romantic anti-capitalism', shaped intellectually by the influences of Weber, Marx, Dilthey, Simmel, Bergson, and others, into communism. Lukács joined the newly formed Hungarian Communist Party at the end of 1918 and played a prominent part in the short-lived Hungarian Commune of 1919. He was to spend the rest of his life in the international Communist movement.

Lukács's early Marxism was profoundly shaped by his prerovolutionary 'romantic anti-capitalism'. Michael Löwy has written of his

> fervent messianism . . . theoretically grounded in the view that the proletariat bears a new harmony, a rediscovered totality, a universal made real, and a reconstituted unity of subject and object, ethics and praxis, individuality and collectivity. Here, tragic nostalgia for a mythical golden age of the past is transformed into passionate hope in the future – hope that the proletariat, as the messiah-class of history, will secure the world's redemption through the path of revolution.[40]

Although Lukács had sloughed off the more extreme versions of this messianism – a refusal typical of the 'left' Communists to consider any tactical compromises such as working in reformist trade unions or standing candidates in bourgeois elections – by the time he wrote (or rewrote) *History and Class Consciousness*, the book still bears its mark, above all in the notion that the working class is the 'identical subject-object' of history.[41]

Consider, for example, the way in which Lukács sought to reappropriate the mantle of orthodoxy from Kautsky. 'Orthodox Marxism', he wrote, 'is not the "belief" in this or that thesis, nor the exegesis of a "sacred" book. On the contrary, orthodoxy refers exclusively to *method*.' (*HCC* 1.) And what does this method consist in? 'It is not the primacy of economic motives in historical explanation that constitutes the decisive difference between Marxism and bourgeois thought, but the point of view of totality . . . *The primacy of the category of totality is the bearer of the principle of revolution in science*.' (Ibid. 27.) Earlier Marxists, for example, Labriola, had argued that the starting point of historical materialism was the concept of the social whole, attacking attempts to resolve social formations into sets of discrete factors. But they tended to attribute to the totality a hierarchical structure, such that the level of development of the productive forces determined the relations of production, and the relations of production the superstructure. For Lukács, on the other hand, society is a totality because it is the creation of a total subject:

> Reality can only be understood and penetrated as a totality, and only a subject which is itself a totality is capable of this penetration. It was not for nothing that the young Hegel erected his philosophy on the principle that 'truth must be understood and expressed not only as substance but also as subject'. (Ibid. 39.)

The role of total subject, of 'the identical subject-object of the social and historical process of evolution' could only be assumed by the proletariat (ibid. 149).

Lukács sought to explain why this was so through his theory of reification. He took over from Max Weber the belief that Western society is characterized by a tendency towards rationalization — the fragmentation of work in order to achieve the maximum output, the replacement of traditional values based on personal loyalties with 'rational-legal' systems of formal rules, the bureaucratization of both public and private sectors, the pervasive spread of an 'instrumental rationality' oriented upon finding the most efficient means to achieve given ends.[42] But while Weber believed that rationalization was inherent in large-scale organization and that, therefore, 'the future belongs to bureaucratization',[43] Lukács argued that these tendencies were specific to capitalism and could be explained by Marx's analysis of the fetishism of the commodity (C i. 163–77). The peculiar feature of capitalism is reification, the transformation of social relations, relations between people, into relations between things. This is effected through the exchange of commodities, as a result of which men find themselves ruled by the relations of their products in the market; at the same time, quantity drives out quality, the rich diversity of use-values is reduced to portions of abstract social labour. The source of reification in commodity fetishism explains, Lukács claimed, one very important aspect of rationalization, the way in which it facilitates technical success in the pursuit of a specific goal, at the price of any comprehension of the whole. Here is reflected the anarchy of bourgeois society, the inability of the capitalist economy to function except through the fluctuations of supply and demand, bringing boom and slump inevitably in its wake.

The same inability to comprehend reality as a whole is characteristic of bourgeois thought, Lukács argued. Classical philosophers have either merely transcribed the surface appearance of reality, conceived as a collection of stray facts, the inner structure an unknowable thing-in-itself, or mystified the totality, transforming it into the Absolute, and thereby detaching theory from practice, turning thought into the retrospective reconstruction of Spirit's path through the world. Only the proletariat can comprehend society as a historically evolved totality, because the heart of reification lies in the transformation of the worker into a thing, of labour-power into a commodity. The working class is, in other words, the identical subject-object of bourgeois society, both an absolute object, deprived of any human status, and at the same time the core of the mediations constitutive of the totality. 'Historical materialism', in which the proletariat becomes conscious of itself, is also 'the *self-knowledge of capitalist society*' (*HCC* 299) because of the pivotal position occupied by workers within bourgeois relations of production. Marxism derives its objective and scientific status from the role it plays in articulating the consciousness of the proletariat, the universal class which 'cannot liberate itself as a class without simultaneously abolishing class society as such' (ibid. 70).

History and Class Consciousness represents the most ambitious attempt to reintroduce the concept of a transcendental subject into Marxism. The Austro-Marxists had contented themselves with the claim that, in Adler's words, 'the basis of all sociation can only be found in individual consciousness'.[44] Lukács, however, accorded to a collective subject, the proletariat, the status of the Hegelian Absolute Idea: as he later put it, 'it appears as if the logico-metaphysical construction of the *Phenomenology of Mind* had found its authentic realization in the existence and the consciousness of the proletariat.' (*HCC* xxiii.) The intellectual impact of *History and Class Consciousness*, and especially of the analyses it contained of reification and of class consciousness, was enormous. By the end of the 1920s it occupied, with Heidegger's *Being and Time* and Mannheim's *Ideology and Utopia*, the centre stage of philosophical discussion in Germany. At the same time, Lukács, along with Karl Korsch, who expressed similar, if cruder views in his *Marxism and Philosophy* (1923), had to endure a savage roasting for 'idealism' at the hands of their fellow Communists. They were even selected for specific mention and condemnation by Zinoviev at the Fifth Congress of the Communist International in June 1924: 'we cannot tolerate such theoretical revisionism in our Communist International,' he declared.[45]

It was, however, less these institutional pressures within the Comintern, then in the process of being first 'Bolshevized' and then Stalinized, than awareness of its conceptual difficulties which motivated Lukács's rejection of *History and Class Consciousness*. The book's fascination lies in its impossibility, its 'attempt to out-Hegel Hegel', as Lukács later put it (*HCC* xxiii), the way in which he seems in it to vacillate between rejecting and succumbing to the thoroughgoing idealism implied by the concept of an absolute subject-object. The proletariat functions in *History and Class Consciousness* as a philosophical category, as it does in Marx's 1843 'Introduction'. But, as one of the book's defenders, Jozsef Révai, asked at the time, is the working class a plausible candidate for the role of absolute subject-object?[46] A class formed and reproduced within capitalist relations of production, brought into being by a historical process, the expropriation of the direct producers, surely the proletariat is as much a creation of bourgeois society as its creator? Moreover, the class struggle stretching from the most elementary economic conflicts to the seizure of power is reduced to a *prise de conscience* on the part of the proletariat, a sudden leap from the status of absolute object to that of absolute subject. Indeed, the proletarian revolution itself seems to be reduced to an act of consciousness: 'since consciousness is not the knowledge of an opposed object, but is the self-consciousness of the object *the act of consciousness overthrows the objective form of its object*' (*HCC* 178). Here the idealist implications of the concept of an identical subject-object are most clearly exposed. Social relations are reduced to forms of consciousness, while ideological struggle is given primacy in the overthrow of capitalism. We are not far here from the young Hegelians.

It must be stressed, however, that *History and Class Consciousness* is a transitional work. The last two essays, 'Critical Observations on Rosa Luxemburg's *Critique of the Russian Revolution*', and 'Towards a Methodology of the Problem of Organization', form a unity with Lukács's little book, *Lenin* (1924). Together these texts represent a marked shift away from the messianism of his early Marxism, and an acceptance of Lenin's 'revolutionary *Realpolitik*'. Thus, the concept of the revolutionary party developed in these essays is that of an organization created by the interaction of theory and practice, vanguard and class, a view much closer to those of Lenin and Gramsci than the Utopian sect embodying the class consciousness 'imputed' to the proletariat of Lukács's earlier writings. Ironically, this convergence between Lenin's thought and Hegelian Marxism (Gramsci was travelling a very similar journey away from Bordiga's ultra-leftism at much the same time) occurred at much the same time as it ceased to be possible to be both a revolutionary and a Realpolitiker. The German October of 1923, regarded by the Bolshevik leadership as the essential complement of their own capture of power, was a farce, presaging the tragedy of the Soviet state. Lukács's essay on Lenin was written in homage after the latter's death in January 1924, at the very moment when Lenin's thought was about to be transformed into 'Leninism', the official ideology of the Soviet state to this day.[47] The cult of Lenin served to legitimize the power of the ruling bureaucracy, whose abandonment of the Bolshevik strategy of world revolution was made explicit in the theory of 'socialism in one country'. For the next two decades, Stalinism and fascism conspired (sometimes consciously) to extirpate the revolutionary wing of the Communist movement. Within little more than two years Gramsci was in Mussolini's prison, within five Trotsky was in exile, and Lukács had made his peace with the Comintern apparatus.

The twin catastrophes of the 1920s and 1930s – the defeat of revolution in the West and its degeneration in the East – scarred even the thought of Trotsky, Stalin's most unflinching Marxist foe. He had told the Third Congress of the Comintern that 'faith in automatic evolution is the most important and most characteristic trait of opportunism'.[48] His writings on fascism in Germany are a brilliant demonstration of the fact that the victory of the working class is not fated, but depends upon political and ideological conditions, such as proletarian consciousness and organization. But isolation and defeat led Trotsky to embrace precisely such a 'faith in automatic evolution'. Launching the fourth International in 1938, he declared that

> the orientation of the masses is determined first by the objective conditions of decaying capitalism, and second, by the treacherous politics of the old workers' organizations. Of these factors, the first is the decisive one: the laws of history are stronger than the bureaucratic apparatus.[49]

The pendant to evolutionism in Trotsky's case was not opportunism but voluntarism: the only obstacle to world revolution was the 'treacherous politics' of Stalinism and social democracy. This coupling of evolutionism and voluntarism was present in Stalinism itself, which combined an identification of socialism with the expansion of the productive forces with a vast overestimation of the ability of backward societies to build socialism irrespective of their material conditions. Evolutionism, systematically expounded in Stalin's 'Dialectical and Historical Materialism', first published as part of that notorious celebration of the Moscow trials, the *History of the CPSU (b) (Short Course)* (1938), guaranteed the triumph of socialism; voluntarism legitimized absurdities such as the post-war 'Great Plan for the Transformation of Nature', and the slaughter of millions whose 'sabotage' was held responsible for all the country's ills. The price was paid not only by the victims of the purges; faith in their ultimate triumph helped justify the German Communists' refusal to fight for a united front against Hitler. In the words of Walter Benjamin, like Trotsky a victim of the triumphant dictators at the darkest moment of the twentieth century, the summer of 1940: 'Nothing has corrupted the German working class so much as the notion that it was moving with the current.'[50] Thereafter, no intellectually serious Marxist could make this assumption.

(3) Critics of Hegel—Adorno and Althusser

It was in this climate of defeat, as Perry Anderson has emphasized, that Western Marxism emerged. The unstable economic and political equilibrium of the 1920s gave way first to the terrible defeats of the 1930s, to Hitler, Franco, and the Great Purges, and then to a Second World War which left the globe divided between two imperialist power blocs. In the West, the working class appeared thoroughly integrated into the system, bought off with cars, fridges, and hire purchase, in the East they were firmly under the boot of the secret police and the Red Army. Serious Marxist work became predominantly academic in origins and tone, philosophical in approach, obsessed with cultural rather than political and economic issues, and generally pessimistic about the prospects for revolution.[51] The chief exceptions to this pattern were the more creative of Trotsky's followers, while Marxists working in specific disciplines made some progress. (This was true, in the English-speaking world, of economics and history.)

Philosophically, Western Marxism represented a radical break with the thought of its predecessors. Up to that time, Marxists had regarded themselves as the intellectual heirs of the Enlightenment. For Marx, as for Condorcet, history *progressed*: beneath the flux of events was an intelligible pattern, the growth of man's ability to control his destiny. The difference between Marx and the *philosophes* was that historical materialism explained progress not as that of the human mind, but as the effect of specific combinations of forces and relations of production. Progress, for Marx, was essentially contradictory, occurring within the framework of relations of exploitation, and motored by the class struggle. He looked forward to the proletarian revolution: 'then only will human progress cease to resemble that hideous pagan idol, who would not drink the nectar but from the skulls of the slain.' (*SW* i. 499.) This complex conception of progress was transformed by Kautsky and the other Marxists of the second International into the irresistible expansion of the productive forces, to which social structures must inevitably adjust. The spiral course history described in Marx, progress taking place through violence and exploitation, was flattened out into a straight line extending indefinitely into the future.

It was against this vulgarized conception of humanity's 'progression through a homogeneous empty time', which he believed disarmed the masses in their struggle against the ruling class, that Benjamin rebelled in his 'Theses on the Philosophy of History' (1940), cited at the end of the preceding section. His image of history seemed to imply the denial of the very concept of progress:

A Klee painting named 'Angelus Novus' shows an angel looking as though he was about to move away from something he is fixedly contemplating. His eyes are staring, his mouth is open, his wings are spread. This is how one pictures the angel of history. His face is turned toward the past. Where we perceive a chain of events, he sees one single catastrophe which keeps piling wreckage upon wreckage and hurls it in front of his feet. The angel would like to stay, awaken the dead, and make whole what has been smashed. But a storm is blowing from Paradise; it has got caught in his wings with such violence that the angel can no longer close them. This storm irresistibly propels him into the future to which his back is turned, while the pile of debris before him grows skyward. This storm is what we call progress.[52]

The 'Theses' had a profound effect on the two leading members of the Frankfurt school, Max Horkheimer and Theodor Adorno. The Frankfurt Institute of Social Research, founded in 1923, had in the 1930s under Horkheimer's directorship operated within a broadly Lukácsian framework: the theory of reification provided the methodology of their critical analyses of bourgeois thought and culture. However, Adorno and Horkheimer both rejected the concept of an absolute subject-object of history. The former wrote in 1931 that 'anyone who chooses philosophy as a profession today must first reject the illusion that earlier philosophical enterprises begin with: that the power of thought can grasp the totality of the real'.[53] At the same time the Frankfurt theorists refused to consider theories as merely expressions of class world-views, insisting that theoretical discourse cannot be reduced to its social conditions of production.[54] The effect, however justified this repudiation of relativism, was a certain distancing of theory and practice reminiscent of the left Hegelians. Horkheimer wrote in 1936 that 'even the situation of the proletariat is, in this society, no guarantee of correct knowledge'; 'critical theory' (as he renamed Marxism) 'has no specific influence on its side, except concern for the abolition of social injustice.'[55]

The detachment of 'critical theory' from the proletariat was completed by the Second World War and the experience in exile of American consumerism. (Benjamin, by contrast, had remained, in his odd, mystical way, a revolutionary to the end, writing shortly before his death that 'the struggling, oppressed class itself is the repository of historical knowledge'.)[56] Two books by Horkheimer and Adorno published in 1947, Dialectic of Enlightenment and Eclipse of Reason, represented a break with the entire Enlightenment tradition. Western civilization's attempt to increase man's control over nature was inseparably bound up with the domination of man over man. The fissure at the heart of capitalist society was no longer that between classes, but the much deeper conflict setting man at odds with nature. Lukács's analysis of reification was dehistoricized, the rationalization characteristic of modern society explained in terms closer to Weber than to Marx. 'Reification is a process that can be traced back to the beginning of organized society and the use of tools.'[57] The most basic impulse of Western thought, towards enlighten-ment, is inseparably bound up with the drive to dominate man and nature, Horkheimer and Adorno argued. Enlightenment, as much as it seeks to demythologize, to dissolve the transcendent and magical into the this-worldly and rational, reflects the mythical fear of the unknown and the different, reducing the qualitative variety of nature celebrated in magic to the homogeneous and quantitative, a process taken to the limit by positivism's reduction of the real to the measurable. It thus reflects a society ruled by the barter principle, the reduction of useful labour to abstract social labour, or relations between people to relations between things. Reason in such a society is instrumental, 'the organ of calculation, of planning; it is neutral with regard to ends; its element is co-ordination.'[58] The constitutive role of the transcendental subject in German idealism is a philosophical gloss on Western civilization's destruction of nature, so that 'all the power of nature was reduced to mere indiscriminate resistance to the abstract power of the subject'.[59] Or, as Adorno later put it in a memorable aphorism, 'the system is the belly turned mind, and rage is the mark of each and every idealism.' (*ND* 23.) The omnipotence of the Idea reflects the urge to conquer and destroy nature.

The critique of Enlightenment was also, therefore, a critique of Hegelian idealism. Indeed, the most philosophically interesting representatives of Western Marxism were united, whatever their other differences, in a rejection of the Hegelian dialectic in all its forms. At this point the concept of *difference* came to play an important role in Marxist philosophy. Reality, it was argued, is inherently heterogeneous; any attempt to reduce it to a homogeneous totality, the expression of some single unifying principle, must be resisted. This theme, already urged by the classical empiricists, has been taken up in the past century by some very different philosophers – Nietzsche, Heidegger, Deleuze, Derrida.[60] Within Marxism it has been presented most explicitly by Galvano Della Volpe and Lucio Colletti.[61] The most interesting explorations of its implications have been those of Adorno and Althusser. Obviously such an approach involved a break with the thought of the early Lukács, for whom 'the primacy of the category of totality is the bearer of the principle of revolution in science'. As Martin Jay has suggested, 'what both Adorno and Althusser together signify is the exhaustion of the problematic introduced into Marxist theory by *History and Class Consciousness*. Both represent the Marxism of a more sober and disillusioned time.'[62]

The point may be illustrated by comparing Lukács's later views with those of Adorno. Lukács's synthesis of Lenin's thought and Hegelian Marxism had been premissed in *Lenin* on 'the actuality of the revolution', a concept whose ambiguity left open whether it referred to the *immediate* prospects of revolution or merely the general possibility of social upheaval inherent in the imperialist epoch. The stabilization of capitalism in the mid-1920s led Lukács to abandon any hopes of revolution in the West, and to accept the doctrine of 'socialism in one country'. The rest of his political career was devoted to the consistent defence of what could be salvaged from the harmonious totality of which he had dreamed in his youth, the reconciliation of Stalinism and bourgeois culture.[63]

Philosophically Lukács shifted from left to right Hegelianism. Under the influence of the Paris *Manuscripts*, he rejected the concept of an identical subject-object and instead sought, in *The Young Hegel* (1948) and his posthumously published *Ontology of Social Being*, to root the dialectic in the interaction of man and nature in the labour-process. The concept of the relations of production, in which the specificity of historical materialism lies, was largely absent from Lukács's later writings. Instead, we have an Olympian conception of history whose mechanisms were modelled on Hegel's *List der Vernunft* (Ruse of Reason). Historical progress is secured through men's self-seeking and apparently irrational actions, even though they are unaware of this inner meaning – a handy explanation of Stalinism, among other phenomena. The task of thought is to reflect this process, to trace what Hegel called 'the rose in the cross of the present', the thread of rationality running through an anarchic world. Literature which refuses this task (for Lukács treated art as a form of knowledge), such as the work of Joyce and Kafka, where reality is depicted as chaotic and irrational, is of no aesthetic merit, mere decadence. For the later Lukács, as for Hegel, 'what is rational is actual and what is actual is rational'.

This 'reconciliation with reality' was anathema to Adorno. He championed aesthetic modernism precisely for its stress on fragmentation, difference, and dissonance, which reflected more accurately than the 'socialist realism' espoused by Lukács a world ruled by commodity fetishism, and which derived from the subject's refusal to be wholly incorporated into this world. Adorno denounced Lukács's assumption that 'the reconciliation has been accomplished, that all is well with society, that the individual has come into his own and feels at home with his world ... But the cleavage, the antagonism persists, and it is a sheer lie to assert that it has been "overcome", as they call it, in the Eastern bloc.'[64]

Adorno declared war *à l'outrance* on the Hegelian theodicy in both its original and Marxist versions, the effacement of difference, and the reconciliation of contradictions in a self-identical whole. The task of philosophy, he believed, was, like Goethe's Mephistopheles, to deny, to negate, and to break down the delusive harmonics of reason, a mission which led Lukács, as a good servant of history, to denounce Adorno for having 'taken up residence in the "Grand Hotel Abyss"'.[65] Adorno saw himself as a champion of multiplicity, of difference:

> The matters of true philosophical interest at this point in history are those in which Hegel, agreeing with tradition, expressed his dis-interest. They are nonconceptuality, individuality, and particularity – things which ever since Plato used to be dismissed as transitory and insignificant and which Hegel labelled 'lazy *Existenz*'. (*ND* 8.)

This rehabilitation of difference had ethico-political connotations. Adorno regarded the Absolute as the philosophical correlate of a society subordinated to commodity fetishism. The reduction of the concrete particular by Hegel to a concept, particularity, in which *the* concept (*Begriff*, Notion, i.e. the Idea) manifests itself, he believed to be symptomatic of the totalitarianism implicit in the exchange of commodities, which reduces the qualitative and individual to mere quantities of abstract social labour. Against Hegel, for whom 'the truth is the whole', Adorno affirmed: 'the whole is the false'.[66] Only the individual subject (not the transcen-dental subject or the absolute subject-object) provides any refuge in a world dominated by commodity fetishism.

Yet Adorno's attitude to Hegel was not one of wholesale rejection. More than any other philosopher perhaps, he conveys a sense of knowing Hegel from the inside, an intimate understanding of the strengths as well as the weaknesses of his system. He was especially struck by Hegel's critique of the Kantian subsumptive judgement, where particulars are treated as external to the universal concepts in which they are included. The notion of the concrete universal, the immanent unity of particular and concept, remained for Adorno the model of knowledge, even if he was aware that Hegel himself had resolved the individual and particular back into the concept. The resulting dilemma was well expressed in this passage from *Minima Moralia* (1951):

> Knowledge can only widen horizons by abiding so insistently with the particular that its isolation is dispelled. This admittedly presupposes a

relation to the general, though not one of subsumption, but rather the reverse. Dialectical mediation is not a recourse to the more abstract, but a process of resolution of the concrete in itself . . . But how much more difficult has it become to conform to such a morality [of thought] now that it is no longer possible to convince oneself of the identity of subject and object, the ultimate assumption of which still enabled Hegel to conceal the antagonistic demands of observation and interpretation.[67]

This dilemma – how to achieve Hegel's goal of grasping the specificity of objects in thought while not, like Hegel, reducing them to moments of the Idea's self-realization – is the theme of Adorno's *Negative Dialectics* (1966). The solution he offered was profoundly influenced by the thought of his mentor, Walter Benjamin, who had, before his conversion to Marxism in the mid-1920s, developed a highly original philosophy of difference.[68] For Benjamin, reality is, as Michael Rosen put it, 'a world of fragments, related to each other like the shards of a smashed pot, each of these entirely unique, and yet, for that, not necessarily isolated'.[69] This conception was completely incompatible with a hierarchical conception of Being as the manifestation of the Idea or as constituted by the subject. 'The eternal', Benjamin wrote in his unfinished masterwork on the Paris of Baudelaire, the *Passagenarbeit* or Arcades Project, 'is more like the lace-trimming on a dress than like an idea.'[70] Yet his stress on the unique and fragmentary did not lead Benjamin to either scepticism or empiricism, but to an extraordinary 'negative theology'. In an early pre-Marxist essay, 'Language as Such and the Language of Man' (1916), he depicted a resonating universe of things communicating with each other. Human language is a developed version of this communication between material objects:

> The translation of the language of things into that of man is not only a translation of the mute into the sonic; it is also a translation of the nameless into the name . . . The objectivity of this translation is, however, guaranteed by God. For God created things; the creative word in them is the germ of the cognizing name, just as God, too, finally named each thing after it was created.[71]

This idea, drawn for Jewish mysticism, that, in the name, word and thing are identical, provided Benjamin with a model of thought even after he became a Marxist. The 'natural correspondences' between things, he wrote in 1931, 'are given their true importance only if seen as stimulating and awakening the mimetic faculty in man', the 'power of seeing resemblances' which is 'a rudiment of the powerful compulsion in former times to become and behave like something else'.[72] But thought is not mimetic in the sense of providing images of things, their visual reproduction. Nor does it subsume them under concepts, classify them, or resolve them into the Idea. Rather it seeks to approach them directly by constructing constellations, configurations of elements drawn from the world of experience but rearranged so as, through their structure, to reveal the correspondences between things. Thought arrives at truth not by mirroring the world, but by participating in it, by sharing its structure; it is, therefore, irreducibly multiple since reality itself is inherently heterogeneous.[73]

Negative Dialectics is remarkable for the manner in which it seeks to transpose this philosophy of difference, already espoused by Adorno in his 1931 inaugural lecture at Frankfurt University, 'The Actuality of Philosophy', into a Hegelian-Marxist framework. 'The thought is not the image of the thing,' he wrote, echoing Benjamin, it rather 'aims at the thing itself' (ND 205). Having rejected the negation of the negation as the triumph of the 'anti-dialectical principle', the reduction of difference to identity, Adorno argues that 'the unifying moment survives without a negation of negation, but also without delivering itself to abstraction [i.e. subsuming judgement which merely includes particulars under a universal without showing their connection] as a supreme principle. . . . Instead, the concepts enter into a constellation. The constellation illuminates the specific side of the concept, the side which to a classifying procedure is either a matter of indifference or a burden.' (Ibid. 158, 162.) Language itself proceeds in such a manner. 'Where it becomes a form of representation, it will not define its concepts. It lends objectivity to them by the relation into which it puts the concepts, centred about a thing.' (Ibid. 162.) Thought attains the status of the name, the identity of word and thing, in so far as the configurations in which its concepts are arranged reproduce the inner structure of specific objects; 'by gathering round the object of cognition, the concepts potentially determine the object's interior.' (Ibid.) 'Without affinity, there is no truth . . . Consciousness knows as much about its otherness as it resembles that otherness.' (Ibid. 270.)

Adorno's adherence to Benjamin's metaphysics of the name

was by no means complete. He insisted against both Benjamin and Heidegger that knowledge involves more than the immediate intuition of bare essences; it requires also the moment of reflection, the conceptualization of the mediations characteristic of a social whole pervaded by commodity fetishism. Here his debt to Lukács's theory of reification, which treats the different aspects of capitalist society as expressions, albeit in an indirect and mediated form, of the transformation of labour-power into a commodity, is evident. He criticized Benjamin's method in the *Passagenarbeit* of assembling 'dialectical images', constellations, comparison of which revealed the direct correspondences between economic and cultural phenomena. He wrote of Benjamin later, 'his micrological and fragmentary method . . . never entirely integrated the idea of universal mediation, which in Hegel, as in Marx, produces the totality.'[74] Adorno thus accepted the concept of totality, not in the sense of the absolute subject-object, but rather because commodity fetishism *produces* a totality, reducing the qualitative diversity of the real to the single homogenous dimension of abstract social labour. 'Even in the theory of the conceptual mediation of all being, Hegel envisaged something decisive in real terms . . . The act of exchange implies the reduction of the products to be exchanged to their equivalents, to something abstract.'[75] The reduction of reality in all its concreteness and variety to the expressions of the Absolute reflects the process of abstraction at work in reality itself, the transformation of concrete, useful labours into abstract social labour inherent in the exchange of commodities. Critical theory must, therefore, preserve a moment of abstraction, of reflection, not allowing the concept of the totality to disintegrate, if it is to fulfil its role of understanding, and demystifying reality.

Yet Adorno's adoption of Benjamin's treatment of thought as mimetic pulls away from the anti-naturalism characteristic of Hegelian Marxism and expressed, for example, in the rejection of a dialectic of nature. The notion shared by Horkheimer, Adorno, and Marcuse that philosophy is comparable to aesthetic experience, in that both permit the reconciliation of man and nature, is traceable to Benjamin, and beyond him to an entire philosophical tradition embracing Kant, Schiller, Goethe, and Schelling. (Benjamin's *Origins of German Tragic Drama* begins with Goethe's saying that 'we must necessarily think of science as art if we expect to derive any wholeness from it'.)[76] The influence of Benjamin and Adorno is evident in this passage by Horkheimer:

Philosophy helps man to allay his fears by permitting language to fulfil its genuine mimetic function, its mission of mirroring the natural tendencies. Philosophy is at one with art in reflecting passion through language and thus transferring it to experience and memory. If nature is given the opportunity to mirror itself in the realm of spirit, it gains a certain tranquillity by contemplating its own image.[77]

This conception, which treats man as part of nature, fits perfectly well into Benjamin's philosophy, which remained resolutely anti-Hegelian in its stress on the profusion and diversity of being, and its refusal to admit the concept of totality. It was less obviously compatible with the sharp division between the natural and social sciences made by Lukács. It would have married better with either Romantic *Naturphilosophie* or naturalistic materialism, both of which treat man and nature as indissolubly united. (Characteristically, Benjamin was attracted to both, and to Surrealism besides.)[78] But the Frankfurt school were perfectly orthodox Lukácsians in this respect, denouncing all those who accepted the methodological unity of the natural and social sciences as 'positivists'.[79] It is, therefore, not surprising that Jürgen Habermas, in attempting to develop Frankfurt Marxism in a more conventionally neo-Kantian direction, should have repudiated the notion of 'the resurrection of nature, . . . no matter how much the early Marx and the speculative minds in the Marxist tradition (Walter Benjamin, Ernst Bloch, Herbert Marcuse, Theodor W. Adorno) find themselves attracted by this heritage of mysticism'.[80]

While Adorno deconstructed Hegelian Marxism from within, Louis Althusser attacked it from without. He did so in a political context very different from that of Frankfurt Marxism, from within the French Communist Party, and under intellectual influences largely alien to the anti-naturalism of the German philosophical tradition – Spinoza's *Ethics,* Saussure's structural linguistics, Lacan's reinterpretation of Freud, Bachelard's philosophy of science.[81] Thus his two most celebrated books, *For Marx* and the collaborative work *Reading Capital,* both first published in 1965, are noteworthy for the stress they lay on the scientific character of Marxism: 'Marx "opened up" for scientific knowledge a new "continent", that of *history* – just as Thales opened up the "continent" of mathematics for scientific knowledge, and Galileo opened up the "continent" of physical nature for scientific knowledge.' (*FM* 14.) Althusser also scandalized the intellectual world by attacking the fashionable interpretation of Marx as a humanist thinker, a view supported by liberal and social-democratic commentators, but also taken up by the Communist Parties especially after Khrushchev's denunciation of Stalinism in 1956: against this, Althusser asserted that Marx's thought is riven by an 'epistemological break' separating the Paris *Manuscripts* from the scientific works of his maturity.

To prove his point, Althusser had to show that there was a fundamental difference between the Marxist and Hegelian dialectics. His critique of Hegel, first developed in the celebrated essay 'Contradiction and Overdetermination' (1962), was more radical than Adorno's, for it repudiated not only the identical subject-object, but also the Hegelian method of conceptualizing the social whole retained by the Frankfurt school. Hegel's dialectic, Althusser argued, involves an 'expressive' conception of totality, 'a totality all of whose parts are so many "*total parts*", each expressing the others, and each expressing the social totality that contains them, because each in itself contains in the immediate form of its expression the essence of the totality itself' (*RC* 96). The whole is thus thought to possess some core, some basic principle, of which the other elements of the whole are mere reflections. For example, in the case of Lukács's theory of reification (retained in a modified form by the Frankfurt Marxists), the different aspects of the totality replicate the structure of the basic contradiction, the transformation of labour-power into a commodity; rationalization and fetishism are transmitted throughout the social formation from their core in the relation between capital and labour. The effect, Althusser claims, is to reduce the diversity of social life to mere epiphenomena of the economy. His paradoxical conclusion is that Hegelian Marxism (or 'historicism', as Althusser rather confusingly tends to call it) is just as reductionist, just as dismissive of cultural and political phenomena, as evolutionist Marxism. The latter accords primacy to the productive forces, the former to the transformation of labour-power into a commodity; in either case, ideological and political relations are epiphenomena of the economy.

Like Adorno and Della Volpe, Althusser regarded multiplicity, difference, as primordial. 'Marxism rejects . . . the theoretical presupposition of the Hegelian model: the presupposition of an original simple unity . . . There is no longer any original simple unity. . . , but instead, *the ever-pre-givenness of a structured* complex unity.' (FM 198-9.) Or, as Althusser's collaborator, Étienne Balibar, put it, 'a *plurality* of instances must be an essential property of every social structure' (RC 207). The problem of how a 'plurality of instances' combines to form a 'complex structured unity' was obviously crucial once Althusser had rejected the Hegelian notion of 'expressive totality'. His critics accused Althusser of resolving society into an aggregate of discrete elements lacking any intrinsic connection to one another. His reply was 'to claim that *the complex whole has the unity of a structure articulated in dominance*' (FM 202). In other words, every social formation is constituted by a 'structure in dominance', a specific hierarchial organization of the social practices composing it such that one of them plays the dominant role. Thus, in feudalism the political instance is dominant, in capitalism the economic itself. The economy is, however, always *determinant in the last instance,* since which aspect of the whole is dominant depends upon the nature of the prevailing relations of production. The causality of economic relations is indirect, operating only via the complex of social practices forming the structure in dominance. Contrary to both Hegelian and evolutionist Marxism, ideological and political relations are not epiphenomenal, but constitutive of the social whole. 'The economic dialectic is never active *in the pure state* . . . From the first moment to the last, the lonely hour of the "last instance" never comes.' (Ibid. 113.) A revolutionary rupture is the product, not of 'natural necessity' à la Kautsky, but of an 'overdetermined' accumulation of contradictions involving superstructural as well as economic factors.

This account of the social whole permitted Althusser to claim that the superstructure is 'relatively autonomous' of the economic base, and to criticize the notion of 'a *continuous and homogeneous time*' (RC 99) in terms reminiscent of Benjamin's 'Theses on the Philosophy of History'.[82] Such a stress on the dislocations between the different levels of the social totality was attractive to Althusser for, among others, political reasons. As a member of the French Communist Party critical of Stalinism he wished to be able to explain the 'Stalin phenomenon' in political and ideological terms, crudely, as a survival of bourgeois ideology (see FM 115-16), while continuing to regard the relations of production as socialist. At the same time, Althusser's critique of the reductionism characteristic, on his account, of both evolutionist and Hegelian

Marxism, provided him with impeccable Marxist reasons for asserting the independence of theoretical work from Party control, a matter of some importance to Communist intellectuals after the experience of Zhdanovism and the 'class line' in science at the height of the first cold war.[83]

'Theoretical practice' occupied, indeed, a central position within Althusser's system. He distinguished four instances, or types of social practice, as characteristic of class societies: the economic, political, ideological, and theoretical. All were subsumed under a general concept of practice, derived from Marx's analysis of the labour-process in *Capital* Volume i: 'by *practice* in general I shall mean any process of *transformation* of a determinate given raw material into a determinate *product*, a transformation effected by a determinate human labour, using determinate means (of "production").' (*FM* 166.) The Hegelian Marxists had also laid great stress on the concept of social practice, but for them it denoted both the identity of subject and object, and the expressive unity of the social whole; for Althusser, however, heterogeneity is 'ever pre-given', both in the sense that each practice *combines* essentially distinct elements, and in the sense that the social formation always comprises a multiplicity of practices. This conception of practice is a fundamental challenge to the notion, basic to Hegelian Marxism (and anti-naturalism generally) that society is the creation of the subject.[84] Applied to theoretical discourse, this model of practice involved the claim that the 'means of production', or problematic, of a given discourse, 'the system of *questions* commanding the *answers* given' by the discourse (*FM* 67, n. 30), sets to work, not on reality (the 'real object'), but on the 'thought-object', i.e. the pre-existing concepts and theories in the field. This conception of the sciences operating entirely 'in thought', according to their own internal norms ('*theoretical practice* is indeed its own criterion, and contains in itself definite protocols with which to *validate* the quality of its product' (*RC* 59)), was heavily influenced by Gaston Bachelard, as was the proposition that the sciences are constituted not through generalization from experience, but through a *break* with experience, identified by Althusser with ideology, which he treated, not as Marx had, as the reflection of a contradictory and exploitative reality, but as 'the *lived* relation between men and their world', 'a structure essential to the historical life of societies', even communism (FM 233, 232).[85]

Althusser described his reinterpretation of historical materialism as a 'return to Marx', not to the ideological, humanist Marx of the Paris *Manuscripts*, but the scientific, materialist Marx of *Capital*. At stake in this 'return' was an attempt to reinstate the concept of the class struggle at the heart of Marxism. This is the significance of Althusser's declaration that '*history is a process without a subject*'.[86] Like Adorno, Althusser rejected any attempt to secularize Hegel's theodicy, to treat history as the realization of any predetermined end, the manifestation of any subject, transcendental or collective. But, whereas Adorno had taken refuge in the individual as the only space not yet completely subjugated by commodity fetishism, Althusser sought to restore the stress laid in *Capital* on the relations of production as objective, antagonistic structures determinant of social life. Thus he attacked humanist interpretations of social relations as intersubjective relations, forms of consciousness. (We have seen an example of such an interpretation in the case of the Austro-Marxists in Section 1 above.) '*The social relations of production are on no account reducible to mere relations between men, . . . to intersubjectivity. . . .* For Marx, the social relations of production do not bring *men alone* onto the stage, but the *agents* of the production process and the *material conditions* of the production process, in specific "combinations".' (*RC* 174.) Especially in his later writings, Althusser stressed that the 'subject' of history is not the Idea, or man, or even the proletariat, but the *class struggle*, whose nature depends on the prevailing relations of production but whose outcome cannot be determined from advance.

However, this attempt to develop a non-teleological version of Marxism was conceptualized in terms whose effect was to make the relations of production eternal, transforming them into unchanging structures. Thus, Althusser treated subjectivity as a necessary illusion generated by ideology which, by giving individuals a false belief in their uniqueness and autonomy, helped to bind them to the status quo.[87] What Adorno and the early Lukács would have regarded as peculiar to a society governed by commodity fetishism, the domination of individuals by anonymous structures, Althusser declared to be an invariant feature of every social formation. Ideology was no longer the site and effect of class struggle, but a factor of social cohesion, the cement of social life: '*ideology (as a system of mass representa-*

tions) is indispensable in any society if men are to be formed, transformed and equipped to respond to the demands of their conditions of existence.' (FM 235.)[88] This picture of history as a closed system was reinforced by a tendency, most clearly evident in Althusser's concept of 'structural causality', to treat social formations as endowed with the capacity to generate their own ideological and political conditions of existence, and therefore to reproduce themselves in perpetuity. Contradictions were conceived as the *effects* of self-sufficient structures, an approach whose implication was to rule out the very possibility of social change.[89]

Beyond these difficulties, which Althusser sought, on the whole unsuccessfully, to resolve in his later writings, was a tendency, which he shared with Adorno, to separate theory from the class struggle. Marxist philosophy, the 'theory of theoretical practice', was accorded the grandiose role of guaranteeing the scientificity of Marxism thanks to its ability to express 'the essence of theoretical practice, through it the essence of practice in general, and through it the essence of transformations, of the "development" of things in general' (FM 169).[90] As for the problem of the unity of theory and practice, this was no problem, since theory itself is a practice, theoretical practice. Marxism became a closed system, without any intrinsic connection to the working class. Adorno's rejection of any attempt to unite theory and practice was more explicit. 'A practice indefinitely delayed is no longer the forum for appeal against self-satisfied speculation; it is merely the pretext used by executive authority to choke, as vain, whatever critical thoughts the practical change might require.' (ND 3.) Althusser, albeit a much more orthodox Marxist than Adorno, basically agreed. Looking back on *For Marx* and *Reading Capital* ten years after their publication, Althusser explained that all he had tried to do was 'justify the relative autonomy of theory and thus the right of Marxist theory not be treated as a slave of tactical decisions'.[91] Both Althusser and Adorno identified practice with Stalinism, and consequently sought to protect theory from its depredations. Their respective political stances, loyal albeit critical membership of the French Communist Party, and effective abstention from politics, implied a shared belief that there was no alternative revolutionary practice to Stalinism. Hence their clashes with the student movement of the late 1960s. The identification of Marxism with the working class, first made in 1843–44, and then developed systematically by Lukács, no longer held.

It does not follow that the balance-sheet of anti-Hegelian Marxism is wholly negative. On the contrary, after Adorno and Althusser it is difficult to take seriously an interpretation of Marx as merely 'inverting' the Hegelian dialectic. The function of the negation of the negation, hailed by Engels and Lukács as the corner-stone of the materialist dialectic, is to heal the wound of difference in Being, to restore the essentially spiritual unity of the Notion, to dissolve the finite material world into the infinite Absolute. This category, and the rest of the conceptual machinery of Hegel's *Logic*, are completely incompatible with materialism. With Adorno and Althusser the concept of difference, of the irreducible heterogeneity of the material world, is domesticated with Marxism. But this achievement is one of destruction. The inconsistencies in their theoretical systems, some of which we have discussed, make complete agreement with either Adorno or Althusser impossible. The rest of this book will be devoted to exploring some of the ways in which Marxism, given the bankruptcy of evolutionism and the subversion of Hegelianism, can be regarded as a coherent materialist philosophy.

4. Materialism and Naturalism

(1) Naturalism and Anti-naturalism

We are now in a better position to understand the sense in which Marxism, in the course of its history, has returned to philosophy. It is not so much that on specific occasions Marxist theoreticians have found themselves grappling with issues which philosophers would regard as belonging to their domain – Lenin's *Materialism and Empirio-Criticism* is such a case. The connection runs deeper: the development of Marxism as a theoretical discourse, and a political practice, is characterized by a series of attempts to justify historical materialism by resort to a wider metaphysical theory, that is, a set of propositions unamenable to empirical verification or falsification. The most important instances are 'dialectical materialism' *à la* Engels, Kautsky and Stalin; Lukács's reintroduction of the transcendental subject into Marxism; and Althusser's 'theory of theoretical practice'. All amount to a restoration of philosophy's traditional role since Descartes, that of *founding* the sciences.

It is interesting to note that this development is in the opposite direction to that taken by the philosophy of the natural sciences. In the latter domain, partly for reasons to which we will advert in the next chapter, attempts to formulate a fundamental ontology, that is, an account of the essential structure of reality, by means of reflection on first principles, conceptual analysis or other *a priori* means, are no longer respectable. It is physics and the other natural sciences which tell us what exists, thereby giving us our fundamental ontology. Philosophers at best try to establish what the different entities have in common, or to economize on them by reducing them to as few kinds of objects as possible. In other words, it is the physical sciences which provide philosophy with its starting-point, and the success of different philosophical accounts is determined by the degree to which they match up to the history and current state of the sciences.[1] Yet it seems as if the reverse is true of Marxism: the validity of historical materialism, as the science of social formations, is dependent on the philosophy, whether evolutionist, Hegelian, or Althusserian, which founds it.

This contrast launches us into deep and murky waters, those in which the status of the social sciences generally is debated. Many philosophers and social scientists, including Marxists belonging to the anti-naturalist tradition (Lukács, the other Hegelians, and, more ambivalently, the Frankfurt School), believe that the different status that philosophy occupies in relation to the social, as opposed to the natural, sciences arises from a fundamental difference between the study of man and that of nature.[2] In my opinion, this belief is false; it was also not shared by Marx.[3] In this chapter I shall try to expound and defend his views. In doing so I shall be attempting to clarify the senses in which Marxism is a materialism. Andrew Collier usefully distinguishes between three types of materialism: ontological, epistemological, and explanatory.[4] This chapter will deal with the first, which concerns the relation between man and nature, human and physical sciences; Chapter 5 will deal with the second, more commonly known to philosophers as realism. Explanatory materialism, the basis of the Marxist science of history, will receive some consideration in the final section of this chapter; I have discussed it at length elsewhere.[5]

The position which I wish to defend here is naturalism. Its character will become clearer when we consider a number of theses that are candidates for inclusion in this doctrine. Let us commence with the following:

(1) man, as primarily a physical and biological being, is a dependent part of nature;

(2) the methodological principles relevant to the formulation and evaluation of theoretical discourses are the same in both the natural and social sciences;

(3) the concepts and propositions of the natural sciences provide the social sciences with a model for their own procedure.

The first thesis, which treats man as a natural being, is the least problematic, perhaps because its acceptance does not commit one to very much. It would be difficult for any materialist to reject it, indeed its acceptance may be said to be part of what constitutes materialism, but its acceptance does not commit one to materialism. Both Schelling and Feuerbach believed that human reason merely rendered explicit, brought to light, the blind principle at the heart of nature; the history of man was the story of nature's self-expression. Yet Schelling had a romantic conception of nature, while Feuerbach tended, especially in his later years, to mechanistic materialism. At any rate, Marx certainly accepted (1). He wrote in the 1844 *Manuscripts* that 'history itself is a *real* part of *natural history* – of nature developing into man' (*CW* 3:303-4). This conception of man, fundamentally opposed to Hegel's view of nature as the self-estrangement of Spirit,[6] persisted in Marx's writings even after his break with Feuerbach. Thus, in the 'Critique of the Gotha Programme', he attacked the Lassallean doctrine that 'labour is the source of all wealth and culture' for 'falsely ascribing *supernatural creative power* to labour': 'labour is *not the source* of all wealth. *Nature* is just as much the source of use-values (and it is surely of such that material wealth consists!) as labour, which itself is only the manifestation of a force of nature, human labour-power.' (*SW* iii. 13.)

Such a view, supported by a number of passages in *Capital*, of labour as a *co-operative process* between man and nature is important for a number of reasons. First, as we saw in our discussion of Althusser in the previous chapter, it is incompatible with the notion of a subject constitutive of social reality; rather, it highlights the heterogeneity of social relations, involving as they do the combination of distinct elements (labour, raw materials, means of production) in order to produce use-values. The 'subject' of history is the labour-process, and the historically specific relations of production within which it is always already organized.

Secondly, the belief that the labour-process involves an essentially collaborative relationship between man and nature lends support to the attacks made by the Frankfurt school and, in more recent years, by Sebastiano Timpanaro, on the version of Marxism which, in line with one of the main trends of Western thought, treats nature as mere passive raw material, grist to the mill of man's expanding control of his environment, a victim to be conquered, mastered. Horkheimer and Adorno memorably urged that man himself is part of nature, that the capacities which enable him to transform his environment are those of a natural being, and that the refusal to recognize these truths will lead to a terrible revenge on nature's part, ecological catastrophe and the explosive and irrational release of the natural impulses bottled up within people.[7] The issues raised here, which have become more urgent in the last decade with the rise of 'ecopolitics', are too complex to be dealt with here. They were first broached within Marxism by Walter Benjamin, who, with admirable balance, repudiated the notion of man's mastery over nature ('Who would trust a cane-wielder who proclaimed the mastery of children by adults to be the purpose of education?') while refusing to commit the disastrous error into which Adorno and Horkheimer later fell of locating the source of this urge to conquer and destroy nature, not in capitalist relations of production, but in technology.[8]

Let us note finally of (1) that it does not imply the basic proposition of historical materialism, the explanatory primacy of the relations and forces of production. Timpanaro is, therefore, simply mistaken when he writes that 'many (though not all) of the difficulties one encounters in any study of the relationship between [economic] structure and superstructure . . . can be overcome by taking into account the persistence of certain biological data even in social man.'[9] It is perfectly possible to be a materialist in Timpanaro's sense of recognizing 'the physical nature of the [human] subject, . . . and the physical nature of his activities traditionally regarded as "spiritual"',[10] and at the same time to approach society in psychologistic and/or individualistic terms. Indeed, such a combination is characteristic of one trend in bourgeois social thought from Hobbes to behaviourism. Stressing man's irreducible physical and biological basis may be a useful corrective to the idealist excesses of Hegelian Marxism or post-structuralism, but (1) will not yield historical materialism without additional premises.[11]

(2) The Irreducibility of the Social

It is with the second of our theses, that of the methodological unity of the sciences, that the real debate between naturalism and anti-naturalism begins. Unfortunately, serious discussion within Marxism of the issue has been largely vitiated by the extremely crude and inaccurate picture of mathematics and the natural sciences current among Hegelian Marxists and the Frankfurt school. Accounts, for example, of 'science' as the random accumulation of isolated facts reflect both an ignorance of the method and content of the natural sciences, and a willingness to take empiricist philosophy of science at its face-value. Similarly, the critique of the quantifying methods of post-Galilean physics as a reflection of the rationalizing and reifying tendencies of modern society involves a basic incomprehension of the manner in which the mathematization of nature characteristic of the seventeenth-century scientific revolution permitted for the first time the exploration of the inner structure of the physical world, leaving aside the gross reductionism which treats the evolution of modern physics as a manifestation of commodity fetishism. The work of philosophers and historians of science such as Bachelard, Burtt, Canguilheim, Cavaillès, Clavelin, Feyerabend, Foucault, Jacob, Koyré, Kuhn, Lakatos, Popper, and Zahar has demolished the picture of science accepted by empiricists and anti-naturalists alike, replacing it with one in which it is the elaboration of concepts which precedes and guides empirical research. The discussions of the natural sciences in Lukács and the Frankfurt school reflect a common attitude among German philosophers at the turn of the nineteenth century. Sidney Hook reported after a visit to Germany at the end of the 1920s:

> Save for the neo-Kantians and positivist disciples of Mach, all schools are amazingly indifferent to the methods and results of modern physical science. Germany has been the home of the most revolutionary developments in atomic physics, but more excitement has been produced in philosophical circles in England and America by the work of Planck, Heisenberg, Schrödinger, and others than among the generality of German philosophers. . . . The attitude of the German philosopher to science is not always one of indifference. It is often a matter of open hostility.[12]

It is symptomatic of this divide between German philosophy and the natural sciences that the two most important Marxist philosophers reared in this tradition, Lukács and Adorno, wrote copiously on aesthetic theory, but ignored developments in physics.

It is tempting to dismiss anti-naturalism as a symptom of the decline of the German intelligentsia,[13] or as an irrationalist Romantic rejection of science and technology *tout court*.[14] To do so would, however, be too hasty. There is a rational kernel in anti-naturalism, which lies not in its anti-scientism, or its rejection of the methodological unity of the sciences, but in its hostility to (3), the proposition that physics provides the model for explaining social behaviour. The issue is obscured by the belief of anti-naturalists (and many naturalists) that (2) implies, or is equivalent to (3). The theses are, however, distinct. (2) merely commits one to the belief that the social and natural sciences are the same type of enquiry, and that the theories formulated within them must meet the same standards. We shall try to clarify this claim later in this section, but it is worth noting here that Marx made it amply plain in *Capital* that he regarded himself as engaged in precisely the same enterprise as natural scientists, namely that of penetrating beneath the surface appearances of things to reveal the inner structure of reality. For example, he wrote that 'a scientific analysis of competition is possible only if we grasp the inner nature of capital, just as the apparent motions of the heavenly bodies are intelligible only to someone who is acquainted with their real motions, which are not perceptible to the senses' (*C* i. 433).

The methodological unity of the sciences, in the sense in which Marx championed it, does not require that the concepts and proposition used in explaining social behaviour be identical to, or be modelled upon, those constituting the physical sciences. To see more clearly why this is so, let us consider two more theses, sometimes identified with naturalism:

(4) the only complete and satisfactory explanation of human behaviour would consist in the reduction of the social sciences to the physical sciences;

(5) social behaviour must be explained as the manifestation of certain dispositions inherent in human nature.

I shall discuss (5) at greater length in the concluding section of this chapter. It can be rendered consistent with (4) on the assumption that invoking human dispositions provisionally explains social behaviour, prior to the reduction of these dispositions ultimately to physical terms. Historically, the more important connection is between (3) and (5). We saw how in the eighteenth century the triumphs of Newtonian physics provided the Enlightenment with a model of how to explain human conduct. The resulting extension of the methods of physics to the study of man conceived as a *moral* science, that of man as a mental being, led to a psychological account of human nature involving the identification of enduring features of the mind which underlie the varieties of behaviour. 'It is sufficient to my purpose', Hume wrote, 'if I made it appear that, in the production and conduct of the passions, there is a certain regular mechanism, which is susceptible of as accurate a disquisition, as the laws of motion, optics, hydrostatics, or any other part of natural philosophy.'[15] Hume's friend Adam Smith applied this method to political economy, explaining the development of the division of labour as 'the necessary, though very slow and gradual consequence of a certain propensity in human nature . . . the propensity to truck, barter, and exchange one thing for another'.[16]

Before discussing the extent to which Marx himself dealt in such propensities, we must dispose of (4), the demand for a reduction of the human sciences to physics. This proposition, sometimes known as physicalism, is, in a slightly different form, the stuff of contemporary debate in analytical philosophy of mind, which is much concerned with such issues as whether or not the mind (a 'spirit') and the brain (a physical object) are identical. If they are, then it might seem that physicalism holds, and the human sciences may be reduced to neurophysiology. I shall not consider the problem of mind-brain identity here, but will instead concentrate on (4) as a claim as to how human behaviour is to be explained. Let us take W. V. O. Quine's version of the thesis: 'causal explanations of psychology are to be sought in physiology, of physiology in biology, of biology in chemistry, and of chemistry in physics.'[17] It should be noted, first of all, that this claim amounts to the proposal that the human sciences be reduced to physics, only if the former are conceived as *mental* sciences, so that the workings of the individual mind are treated as basic to these disciplines; as I pointed out at the end of the previous section, such an assumption is quite common. It was made possible by the Cartesian identification of the human with the mental. Was Marx a physicalist? There is a passage in the Paris *Manuscripts* which might suggest this: 'natural science will in time incorporate into itself the science of man, just as the science of man will incorporate into itself natural science.' (*CW* 3:304.) The second half of this sentence, however, undermines any attempt to attribute physicalism to Marx, since it appears to suggest that the unification of the sciences will involve a transformation of physics, rather than a reduction of all the other sciences to it. Marx's hope of a unified science, echoed by Adorno, is based on the belief that man, through his labour, will not only realize his own nature, but also humanize nature; it may be a Utopian hope, but it has little to do with physicalism. Again, when Marx wrote that in *Capital* 'the development of the economic formation of society is viewed as a process of natural history' (C i. 92), the context makes it clear that he meant, not that history is explicable in terms of physical laws, but that it is objective, operating independently of the consciousness and will of individual agents.

There are, in any case, at least two good reasons for believing that Marxism and physicalism are incompatible. In the first place, Marx argued that what sets man off from the rest of the natural world is his ability to act upon and transform his natural environment in an indefinite number of different ways. On the basis of this metabolism between man and nature there arise structures which in their complexity and capacity for internally generated transformation are unique to human beings, on this planet at any rate. While this process is only possible by virtue of capacities possessed by man as one among many natural species, once commenced, it is irreversible, short of the destruction of humanity (perhaps not such a remote prospect), and is governed by the laws relating to the historically evolving social relations bound up with the interaction between man and nature in the labour-process. These laws presuppose those at work in the physical world, but are not reducible to them; human history is the process through which human beings, thanks to the development of their productive powers, acquire a certain autonomy of their natural environment, and are able, by virtue of this development and the scientific knowledge bound up with it, to enjoy some degree of control over this environment. Let us note that this argument, if valid, does not prove that physicalism is false; rather, it establishes that if Marxism is true, then physicalism is false. Establishing the truth or falsity of Marxism is another, empirical matter. At any rate, Marx had this argument in mind when he attacked 'the abstract materialism of natural science, a materialism which excludes the historical process' (C i. 494, n. 4).

The second reason for rejecting physicalism is this. As we saw in Chapter 2, Marx believed that man's ability to engage in redirective activity, that is, to perform more than a fixed and limited set of tasks, to set himself qualitatively new goals, is inseparably connected to his capacity to reflect upon his activities, and, indeed, on his reflections. Now, if we accept, as Marx certainly did ('language is as old as consciousness,' he wrote, 'language *is* practical, real consciousness that exists for other men as well' (*CW* 5:44)), that thought and language are similarly inseparable, then certain consequences follow. In particular, one dimension of explaining human conduct is that of *interpretation*, in other words, of assigning a definite sense to the sounds an individual utters, the marks he or she makes on paper. As the work of contemporary analytical philosophers, and especially Donald Davidson, has shown, interpretation is in principle a highly complex process. As we shall see in the following chapters, assigning a sense to the sentences uttered by an individual is bound up with attributing beliefs to him or her. Further, we are unlikely to succeed in giving a sentence the correct sense, or attributing the right belief, without reference to other sentences and beliefs, and without introducing considerations concerning the interpretand's rationality. Even though, Davidson argues, every mental event possesses a physical description (say, as a brain-state) under which it may be explained by the physical sciences, *qua* mental event it cannot be so explained, for the attribution of the belief, intention, desire, or whatever makes it a mental event depends on the complex of other beliefs etc. one attributes to the interpretand, and upon the assumption that he or she is rational, in senses to be specified below.[18]

This second argument against physicalism might seem to allow anti-naturalism in by the back door just after it has been shown out through the front. For just such an argument against (4) has been used at least since Herder to justify rejecting (2), the methodological unity of the sciences. The role of interpretation, anti-naturalists from Dilthey to Gadamer have argued, means that understanding human behaviour is more like reading a book than explaining an ellipse.[19] Nevertheless, interpretation is inescapable in any social enquiry. Unpalatable though this may be for an anti-humanist of Althusserian or post-structuralist persuasion, any description of social practices makes irreducible reference to human beliefs and intentions; whatever else we may want to say about a factory or a prison, it is an institution whose existence depends upon the intentional activities of human beings. Such is the rational kernel of Max Weber's conception of sociology as 'a science concerning itself with the interpretive understanding of human action'.[20]

Marx was well aware of the intentional character of human action: 'man makes his life-activity itself the object of his will and consciousness,' he wrote in the Paris *Manuscripts*, 'conscious life-activity distinguishes man immediately from animal life-activity.' (*CW* 3:276.) He refused, however, to take the further step advocated by Weber (but not, perhaps, consistently pursued by the latter in his substantive work), namely, that of treating the intentions, beliefs, and desires motivating actions as both the *explanans*, and the *explanandum* of social enquiry. On such an approach, having identified some physical movement as an intentional action, we then explain it by specifying the particular beliefs and desires which caused it. (I assume without argument throughout this chapter than human actions are caused.) Marx, by contrast, refused to take intentional activity at its face-value. This was both because of his view that explanation of necessity proceeds by penetrating beneath the observable surface of things to the inner essence – 'all science would be superfluous if the outward appearance and the essence of things coincided' (*C* iii. 817) – and because Marx believed there to be a systematic discrepancy between the way individual agents perceived the capitalist mode of production, and its actual working: 'the final pattern of economic relations as seen on the surface, in their existence and consequently in the conceptions by which the bearers and agents of these relations seek to understand them, is very different from, and indeed quite the reverse of, their inner but concealed essential pattern and the conception corresponding to it.' (Ibid. 209.) Historical materialism is thus concerned with identifying the hidden structures underlying the conscious behaviour of individuals.

Let us consider some of the arguments for saying, *contra* Marx, that the intentional character of human action undermines the methodological unity of the sciences as they are presented in the writings of a philosopher who bridges the analytical and hermeneutic traditions, Charles Taylor. One of his claims is comparatively easy to dispose of, namely, that there is no sharp distinction between theory and 'brute' empirical data in the social sciences.[21] This is indeed true, but, as we shall see in the following chapter, the same can be said of the physical sciences: *all* theoretical discourse is underdetermined by the empirical evidence supporting it. It is surprising to see as sophisticated a philosopher as Taylor naïvely accepting a logical empiricist account of the natural sciences. More recently, he has preferred instead to argue that 'in the sciences of man, the experience of subjects plays an indispensable role, insofar as what people believe and desire, what they admire and condemn figure essentially in explanation.'[22] Interpretation involves a grasp of the interpretand's 'desirability-characterizations' which express these judgements of belief and desire, admiration, and condemnation. Desirability-characterizations are 'inextricably' and 'strongly evaluative' in the sense of being 'normative for desire', telling us what it is right to desire.[23] Taylor then presents social scientists with a dilemma, depending on whether or not they are prepared to give a realist account of evaluative discourse. Realism is here understood in sense (1) of the following chapter: evaluative realism thus claims that an ascription of value 'is capable of being true or false even when the appropriate evidence for or against it is unavailable'.[24] Now, if we reject this doctrine, then we must treat the interpretand's desirability-characterizations as incorrigible. Suttee and slavery would thus turn out to be merely other 'forms of life', undesirable, no doubt, from our own point of view, but not from that of the members of the societies concerned. We would be left, in other words, with what Taylor calls the 'almost mind-numbing relativism' of Peter Winch's *Idea of a Social Science*.[25] If, on the other hand, we accept evaluative realism, and are prepared to regard some of the interpretand's desirability-characterizations as false, then we must give up the idea that the social sciences are value-free. The latter course is recommended by Taylor.

This argument is persuasive, but represents no challenge to Marxism. It is no part of the latter's brief to defend the *Wertfreiheit* of the social sciences; on the contrary, rejection of any such notion is surely inherent in Marxism's claim to provide a *critique* of capitalist society, and of the ideologies which sustain it. Evaluative realism, according to which 'concerning strong evaluations, there is a fact of the matter', as part of a broader challenge to the neo-Kantian doctrine that ascriptions of value are a matter of irreducible subjective choice unamenable to rational criticism and debate, is, if anything, supportive of Marxism, which has always (with the exception of the Austro-

Marxists) denied that there is a gap between fact and value. In the case at issue, Taylor writes, entirely consistently with Marx's refusal to take agents' beliefs and desires at their face-value: 'We have to master the agents' language of self-description and desirability-characterization in order to identify the *explananda* that our theory has to give an account of. . . . But there is no implication in this argument that the language of the agents' understanding must be part of the *explanans*, only that it is basic to the *explanandum*.'[26]

An argument against the methodological unity of the sciences has recently been offered by two followers of Davidson, Graham Macdonald and Philip Pettit.[27] Their starting point is the assumption that explaining a human action depends upon the ascription of rationality to the agent in two senses: first, that his or her actions are an intelligible outcome of a pattern of beliefs and desires (behavioural rationality), and that he or she is responsive to inconsistencies in, and counter-examples to this pattern (attitudinal rationality). This assumption forms the core of what they call the 'orthodox conception of human agents', according to which 'intentional explanation of an action is basic in the sense that other sorts of explanation presuppose it'.[28] Now this conception cannot be revised or replaced in the way in which, for example, Newtonian physics replaced that of Aristotle. The task of the social scientist does not consist in the formulation of general hypotheses which are more adequate than those extant, but in the application to specific cases of the 'indubitable explanatory principles' involved in the 'orthodox conception of human agents'.[29]

The strength of this argument lies in its premiss. It is surely true that social enquiry must treat agents as behaviourally and attitudinally rational. It is doubtful, however, whether it can be *reduced* to the application of this principle. The reason for rejecting this conclusion is that social action is characterized by the existence of regularities which transcend, and indeed systematically constrain the intentional activities of agents – Weber's 'collectivities', Durkheim's 'social facts', Marx's 'social relations'. The specificity of the social, its irreducibility to some more 'fundamental' level, derives from the existence of these regularities. Yet the 'orthodox conception of human agents' treats them as marginal to social enquiry. Some encouragement for this attitude may have been provided by the baneful influence of functionalism on both orthodox social science and Marxism.[30] Functional, or teleological explanations account for a phenomenon in terms of its effects: thus human conduct is explained in terms of its contribution to the reproduction of society. (Althusser's theory of ideology is a good example.) There are good reasons for rejecting both functional explanations in general, in the absence of a specification of the mechanism which permits the *explanandum* to have the effect attributed to it, and functionalism in particular, in the light of its tendency to treat social structures as self-sustaining. It does not follow that one should go to the opposite extreme, and accept methodological individualism, as Macdonald and Pettit do. For this doctrine, which treats social regularities as the unintended consequences of individual actions (a secularized version of Hegel's Ruse of Reason), fails to take note of the way in which these regularities precede, and structure individual choices.

Anthony Giddens offers a middle way between functionalism and individualism by treating social structures as the 'unacknow-ledged conditions and unanticipated consequences' of action, both the 'medium and the outcome of the reproduction of practices'.[31] This formulation is close to Marx's famous statement that 'men make their own history, but they do not make it just as they please; they do not make it under circumstances chosen by themselves, but under circumstances directly encountered, given and transmitted from the past.' (*SW* i. 398.) The weakness of such accounts is that they seem to treat social relations and individual agents as external to each other. To do so gives rise to two problems. First, there is the question of the extent to which human agents are constituted by and within social relations, and therefore cannot be regarded as separable from them. Secondly, and more to the point, Marx tends to treat the relations of production as *generative* of social action. 'Individuals', he wrote at the beginning of *Capital*, 'are dealt with here only insofar as they are the personification of economic categories, the bearers of particular class-relations and interests.' (*C* i. 92.) One might elaborate on this claim as follows. The different lines of conduct available to an agent will depend upon his or her position within the relations of production. The agent is not free to accept or reject this position, and the choices entailed by it: resistance, even the rejection of the existing order, is structured by the relations of production. Individuals can only make the best of the available alternatives. This suggests that explaining human conduct involves more than the ascription of behavioural and attitudinal rationality to agents. What it is rational to do in given circumstances will depend crucially upon the nature of the social context. The link between this context, and the agent's beliefs and desires is provided by the notion of his or her *interests*, and these interests will vary in accordance with the place occupied by the agent within the relations of production – individuals belonging to the same class, therefore, share the same interests. 'Interests' may here be understood thus, following Giddens: 'to say that A has an interest in a given course of action, occurrence or state of affairs, is to say that the course of action, etc., facilitates the possibility of achieving his or her wants.'[32] The imputation of interests to agents on the basis of their class position is an essential component of the process of rendering their behaviour intelligible.

Once rationality has been thus contextualized, there seems to be no good reason why we should seek to formulate generalizations concerning the social regularities which provide the framework of action. Marxism seeks to do so by conceptualizing the different *kinds* of social regularities as modes of production – slavery, feudalism, capitalism, and so on – as a first step to more empirical enquiry. The laws formulated in the course of such investigations are typically statements of *trends*, laws of tendency, rather than deterministic equations involving unique outcomes. Why should not such generalizations, and those formulated within rival research programmes such as neo-classical economics, and Parsonian sociology, be amenable to methodological appraisal in terms of the same standards used to determine the truth or falsity of hypotheses in the natural sciences? The impossibility of constructing artificial experimental conditions in order to test social theories makes the task of their empirical corroboration or falsification more qualitative and approximate than that of physical theories, but does not rule it out *tout court*. As it stands, the issue between Marxism and anti-naturalism turns on the philosophical question of the status accorded to the subject. For if the subject relates to social life as to its own creation, then it is entirely reasonable to conceive of social theory as *self*-knowledge, the rendering explicit of the beliefs and desires motivating individual actions, the explanation of the subjective by the subjective. If, on the other hand, like Marx, one conceives of history as a 'process without a subject', either individual or collective, then social enquiry is likely to focus on the ways in which social relations transcend, and shape human consciousness. At this level, the argument is in my view irresolvable: there is no way of refuting the metaphysical thesis that society is merely the outcome of individual actions, despite its vast empirical implausibility. It is only through the comparison of research programmes embodying this and rival theses that we can hope for a resolution.

(3) Human Nature and the Productive Forces

We are left with (5), the claim that the explanation of social behaviour consists in specifying the persisting features of human nature which given actions manifest. Marx's break with Feuerbach involved his rejection of this thesis as a general methodological principle: 'My analytic method', he wrote, 'does not start from *Man* but from the economically given period of society.'[33] His opposition to (5) was reinforced by his critique of political economy, where he identified the tendency of economists to treat dispositions specific to capitalist relations of production as universal features of human nature (Smith's 'propensity to truck, barter, and exchange' is a good example), and thereby to render natural and unchangeable the characteristics of a temporary and exploitative mode of production. Of course, there is a sense in which Marx was committed to (5). His concept of man as an active, productive being constituted by his labour underlies historical materialism. Yet, as we saw in Chapter 2, Marx ceased in 1845-6 to regard this concept as performing, with the help of a secularized version of Hegel's dialectic, a directly explanatory role; subsequently it shifted to the background. I shall try to clarify the issue by considering G. A. Cohen's recent attempt to give the 'enduring facts of human nature' a higher profile within historical materialism.[34]

Cohen is concerned to vindicate the version of historical materialism expounded in Marx's 1859 Preface to his *Contribution to a Critique of Political Economy* and broadly accepted by the 'orthodox' Marxists of the second International. Here the development of the productive forces is the independent variable in explaining historical change: relations of production are selected according to their capacity to promote the development of the productive forces, while in turn ideological and political relations rise and fall as they favour or impede the survival of the production relations. There are a number of difficulties with this approach, but the one on which I wish to concentrate here centres on the following question: given that it is the expansion of man's productive powers which causes social change, why do 'the productive forces tend to develop throughout history'?[35] To justify this, his 'development thesis', Cohen invokes a transhistorical 'rationality principle', namely, 'rational beings who know how to satisfy compelling wants they have will be disposed to seize and employ the means of satisfaction of these wants': given that men are 'somewhat rational', that their situation is one of scarcity, and that they 'possess intelligence of a kind and degree which enables them to improve their situation', they will expand the productive forces, 'for not to do so would be irrational'.[36]

It is not too difficult to show that this rationality principle cannot play the explanatory role Cohen wishes to give it. For an analysis of a particular mode of production or social formation may reveal that, even though all Cohen's conditions are met, none of the agents of production are disposed to expand the productive forces. A feudal lord, for example, by virtue of the economic power involved in his position as landowner, buttressed by his class's monopoly of the means of coercion, and of the degree of control still exercised by the direct producers over some of the means of production, would be likely to meet an increase in the needs of himself, his family, and his retinue by increasing his peasants' rent, that is, by taking a larger share of a fixed product, rather than by encouraging the producers to increase their output. Similarly, arbitrary and increasing exactions by the lord might deprive his peasants of any incentive to increase the yield of their labour. Indeed, all the evidence suggests that economic growth in the European Middle Ages was extensive, involving an increase in the total amount of land farmed in response to population pressure, rather than a rise in the productivity of labour. Even these periods of growth were followed by catastrophic falls in population and output, suggesting a structural contradiction between relations of production constituted by seigneurial monopoly of land ownership and a labour-process dominated by petty peasant production.[37] Cohen does not consider cases such as these, where the relations of production inhibit the expansion of the productive forces beyond very definite limits, and yet the mode of production in question was able to survive a series of crises spanning several centuries. He does note one example of a catastrophic decline in the productive forces, namely the collapse of the Roman Empire in the West, but only to dismiss it as a case for 'historical pathology' of no interest to 'historical theory', to which the 'development thesis' belongs.[38]

The purpose of my argument is less to deny that the productive forces do, on the whole, develop, than to suggest that the very different forms and rates of expansion can only be explained starting from the relations of production, and treating them, not the forces of production, as the independent variable. Such an approach is much closer to Marx's procedure in *Capital*, where the tendency of capitalism to expand, and indeed constantly to revolutionize the forces of production is explained by the pressure of competition between individual capitals, which forces firms to undertake technological innovations, thereby enabling them to reduce labour costs and undercut their rivals (*C* i. 433-6, *C* iii ch. XV). This account does not of itself vitiate Cohen's version of Marxism: as he points out, 'the bare fact that economic structures [relations of production] develop the productive forces does not prejudice their [i.e. the latter's] primacy, for forces select structures according to their capacity to promote development.'[39] While this is true, if, as I have tried to argue, it is the relations of production which explain the nature and degree of the expansion of the productive forces, then Cohen's development thesis, and the rationality principle it invokes seem redundant. Nor does Cohen's other main claim, the 'primacy thesis', that 'the nature of the production relations of a society is explained by the level of development of the productive forces',[40] seem in a much stronger position. For if at any given time the productive forces expand to the degree, and in the form made possible by the relations of production, it is not clear in what sense the primacy thesis explains anything. If, on the other hand, at certain critical junctures the productive forces override the production relations, bringing into being a new set of relations which will promote the productive forces' further expansion, and this is the image brought to mind by phrases such as 'forces *select* structures', then we are back to full-blooded Kautskyianism, so that social revolutions *must* occur. Indeed, the relegation of aberrant cases where the productive forces decline to 'historical pathology' suggests a view of history as an organic process precisely like that of second International Marxism. Historical progress is inevitable, any sense of the *alternatives* inherent in social struggles, of the possibility of the 'common ruination of the contending classes', is wiped out of Marxism. The result is, however elegant and lucid Cohen's arguments, a notable vulgarization of historical materialism.

It does not follow that Cohen was mistaken in raising the problem of the role played by the 'enduring facts of human nature' in historical materialism. There is no doubt that there are such facts. For example, the capacity of human beings to use language is, in all probability, genetically determined and innate. This does not mean, as Timpanaro seems sometimes to suggest when discussing the biological determinants of human behaviour, that language is a suprahistorical factor, but rather that we must recognize different levels of abstraction, distinguishing between the theoretical models of linguistic capacity constructed by linguistics and philosophical semantics, and the study of the functioning of discourses within definite social formations; in the latter field, Marxism has considerably more to contribute than in the former, as we shall see in Chapter 6.

5. Materialism and Realism

(1) Realism and Marxism

This chapter, like its predecessor, is devoted to clarifying the senses in which Marxism is a materialism. We have seen that one such sense is 'ontological materialism', or naturalism, i.e. thesis (2) of Chapter 4, Section 1, the methodological unity of the sciences. We also saw that for Marx both the natural and the social sciences penetrate beneath the surface appearance of things to a more fundamental reality beneath. Here we shall be concerned with this conception of science. For closely bound up with Marx's naturalism is his 'epistemological materialism', or realism. 'The ideal', he wrote, 'is nothing but the material world reflected in the mind of man, and translated into the forms of thought.' (C i. 102.) It is a similar view of thought as reflecting an independently existing world that Lenin made the essence of materialism, rather than any specific theory of the structure of this world: 'Matter is a philosophical category denoting the objective reality which is given to man by his sensations, and which is copied, photographed and reflected by our sensations, while existing independently of thought.'[1] Materialism thus understood amounts to the epistemological doctrine of *realism* much discussed by contemporary analytical philosophers of language and of science. There seem to be three main elements of this doctrine:

(1) Sentences are true or false by virtue of the state of the world rather than that of human knowledge;

(2) Thought reflects rather than constitutes the world;

(3) The unobservable entities posited to explain the observable behaviour of things exist independently of thought.

Each of these propositions has its own justification. (1) is merely the classical, or correspondence, theory of truth: truth is the *adequatio rei et intellectus*, the correspondence of reality and thought. Its importance in this context lies in its stress on the objectivity of truth: a sentence may be so highly corroborated by the existing standards of science as to be almost self-evident, and yet turn out to be false.[2] (2) is an essential complement to (1), for one might, like Hegel, regard truth as objective, as independent of the subjective certainty that a given sentence is true or false, and yet believe that thought, in the shape of the Absolute Idea, is constitutive of the reality which renders our sentences true or false. Realism in the sense of (2) involves what David-Hillel Ruben calls the 'Independence Claim': 'there are objects essentially independent of all thought, or of all interpretive mental activity.'[3] (3) amounts to the rejection of instrumentalism, that is, of the doctrine that the theoretical entities constructed by the sciences in order to account for the observable phenomena (electrons, relations of production) are conveniences, useful fictions, which permit us to summarize economically the known facts or facilitate the discovery of new ones, involving no commitment as to the existence of these entities. Realism thus understood views the world as stratified, so that the observable behaviour of people and objects is unintelligible unless set in the context of the hidden structures of which it is a manifestation.

Marx would, I think, have accepted all three realist theses. I have already cited on the previous page a passage in which he endorses (2), thought as a reflection of reality, while (3), the contrast between essence and appearance, is of central importance to his procedure in *Capital*. I know of no explicit reference to (1), the objectivity of truth, in Marx's writings, but it is implied in the accounts given by Engels and Lenin of science as a process of infinite approximation to the truth,[4] with which there is little doubt that Marx would have agreed. (We will have more to say on this matter in the concluding section of this chapter.) There would seem to be a conflict between Marx's realism, and the writings of the 1840s, for example, the second thesis on Feuerbach, which states: 'The question whether objective truth can be attributed to human thinking is not a question of theory but a *practical* question. . . . The dispute over the reality or non-reality of thinking is a purely *scholastic* question.' (*CW* 5:3.) Sidney Hook took this passage to amount to the pragmatist doctrine that the truth of a theory consists in its practical efficacy, while Leszek Kolakowski, on the strength of Marx's early writings, has turned him into a transcendental idealist, for whom man seeks to know a world that is his own creation.[5] The 'Theses on Feuerbach' should, however, be placed in their proper context. Marx was rebelling against Feuerbach's conception of the mind as passively registering the movements of external reality. He wished to stress that the world, and above all the social world, can only be known as part of the process of acting upon and transforming it. One may accept this, and still insist that certain distinctions are made. 'Practical efficacy' meant for Marx something much wider than it is normally understood in the pragmatist tradition; it amounts to the capture and retention of political power by the international working class. But the possibility of socialist revolution depends upon the tendencies inherent in the capitalist mode of production towards economic and social crisis. Such tendencies are ascertainable independently of their manifestation in actual crises, since they derive from structural features of capitalism. The objective of *Capital* was to discover these tendencies, 'the economic law of motion of modern society' (*C* i. 92). Possession of a true theory of existing capitalism would permit socialists to anticipate its future development, and hasten its downfall. But this would require some means of determining the truth or falsity of theories independently of their practical efficacy – unless, like Sidney Hook, one believes that the truth of Marx's analysis can only be conclusively established with the triumph of socialism,[6] in which case one has no rational grounds for preferring Marxism to any other research programme. Lenin wrote that 'the Marxist doctrine is omnipotent because it is true':[7] the practical efficacy of Marxism depends upon its truth, rather than being identical to it. Understood thus, there is no conflict between the 'pragmatism' of the 'Theses on Feuerbach', and the realism of *Capital*.

(2) Realism and Essentialism

Recent philosophical discussion in the English-speaking world has seen what Pierre Jacob calls a 'revival of realism',[8] particularly as expressed by the third of the theses considered in the previous section. On this version of realism, which I shall call essentialism, the world is composed of particulars possessing intrinsic natures constituted by certain powers and tendencies; observable reality is the manifestation of these natures and their interactions. There are two main sources of this view. The first, which has had some influence on British Marxists,[9] involves a critique of Hume's analysis of causality. On this account, very widely accepted by analytical philosophers, the causal laws typical of the sciences merely state that some event *a* is constantly accompanied by another event *b*. Any notion of a necessary connection between *a* and *b*, of the sort that common sense normally associates with the statement that *a* caused *b*, is dissolved by this analysis. Causal laws assert the existence of certain regularities among the flux of events. The connection of this treatment of causality to an empiricism which denies existence to anything but the observable should be obvious. It is vulnerable to the Humean problem of induction: how can a generalization which asserts that *a* will always be accompanied by *b* be validly inferred from a necessarily finite number of observations of *a* followed by *b*? The critics of this approach, notably Rom Harré and Roy Bhaskar, argue that such difficulties vanish once we see that such constant conjunctions are the manifestation of the intrinsic natures of powerful particulars. The task of science is to establish what these natures are. Once some well-corroborated hypothesis about the nature of a particular of kind X predicts that in given conditions such a particular will bring about the conjunction *a,b* then *b* must follow *a* in these circumstances *of necessity*. If, in the appropriate conditions, *a* is not accompanied by *b*, then we must suppose either that the circumstances have been misdescribed, or that the hypothesis that attributes the power to bring about *a,b* to particulars of kind X is false. But, provided that the hypothesis is not falsified, then we may say that *a* and *b* are intrinsically connected, bound together by a natural necessity which flows from the essential structure of particulars of the kind in question.[10]

The second development to have lent support to essentialism is the causal theory of names. Here also the starting point is a critique of received doctrine, in this case the standard analysis of proper names and natural-kind words. Whatever their other differences, analytical philosophers as diverse in view as Frege, Russell, Wittgenstein, Strawson, Searle, and Dummett would all agree that the sense of a proper name, say, 'Aristotle', is given by either the conjunction of, or a selection from, a set of definite descriptions, for example, 'the teacher of Alexander', 'the author of the *Nicomachean Ethics*', and so on. Saul Kripke, Hilary Putnam, and Keith Donnellan have challenged this account by, for example, citing cases where we can use a proper name success-fully to refer to someone, even though the definite descriptions we believe to be true of him are false. What is most important for our purposes is that they have extended this critique to natural-kind words, e.g. 'water', 'gold', 'tiger'; that is, to the very class of expressions which on an essentialist account of science denote the entities whose inner structures theoretical enquiry is concerned to discover. According to the causal theory of names, a natural-kind word, like a proper name, first acquires a use, not by having its sense specified in the form of a set of definite descriptions, but by having its reference fixed. This 'initial baptism' may take the form, quite simply, of pointing to a certain animal and saying 'tiger', in circumstances which make it clear that the speaker is giving animals of this sort a name. The reference of the term, once fixed in some such manner, may subsequently change as scientists discover more about the internal structure of particulars of this kind: thus, iron pyrites, 'fool's gold', which might once have been regarded as gold because of its phenomenal properties, has been shown to have a different molecular structure.[11]

Putnam has used this analysis to refute the claims of Paul Feyerabend and Thomas Kuhn that scientific theories are 'incommensurable', i.e. do not refer to the same reality. Their argument was that since the meaning of individual concepts depends on that of the total theory, their meaning will change as the theory does, and so there can be no continuity in the history of sciences, but merely a succession of 'paradigms' offering a different way of viewing the world, none objectively preferable to the others.[12] The causal theory of names seems to allow Putnam to retort that 'meanings ain't in the head'. The correct use of a natural-kind term is not determined by its theoretical context, but depends, first, on some 'introducing event', which fixes its reference indexically, i.e. by picking out some portion of the world as a paradigm case of the particulars falling under this term, and, secondly, on what he calls 'the linguistic division of labour' – the progress of knowledge means that ordinary-language users may often depend upon the judgement of experts to determine whether some purported instance of a natural kind actually possesses the internal structure of particulars of this sort. 'The extension of a term is not fixed by a concept that the individual speaker has in his head, . . . [but] depends upon the actual nature of the particular things that serve as paradigms, and this actual nature is not, in general, fully known by the speaker.'[13]

Unfortunately both the essentialist analysis of causal powers and the causal theory of names share a common weakness: they presuppose a satisfactory realist account of the corroboration of scientific hypotheses. Thus, we can claim that the events whose constant conjunction is predicted by a given causal law are necessarily connected only on the assumption that this law is true; but Harré's and Bhaskar's account of causal powers does not provide any criterion for determining whether this assumption is met. Again, fixing the extension of a natural-kind term presupposes some independent means of corroborating or falsifying hypotheses concerning the internal structure of particulars of that kind. The causal theory of names does not amount to the rebuttal of the claim, made by Kuhn, Feyerabend, and others, that we possess no rational and objective method of deciding between the competing hypotheses which contribute, if the causal account is correct, to determining the reference of natural-kind words. As Richard Rorty has put it, 'our best theory about what we are referring to is merely uncontroversial fall-out from our best theory about things in general.'[14] Unless we can come up with some way of deciding what our 'best theory' is, then essentialism on its own is vulnerable to idealist counter-attack.

(3) Realism and Representation

Realism as we have been discussing it up to now is concerned with what David Papineau calls 'semantico-ontological objectivity', which 'requires that there is an independent reality to which our statements are answerable', as opposed to 'epistemological objectivity', which 'requires the existence of standards which enable people to agree on the relative worth of statements'.[15] Our discussion of essentialism in the previous section suggests that the two types of objectivity are very closely connected: accounts of causal statements and natural-kind terms which support the realist picture of thought mirroring an independent reality turn out to presuppose criteria which enable us to decide our relative degree of success in mirroring this reality.

The rejection of 'epistemological objectivity' along with its 'semantico-ontological' cousin is the common currency of avant-garde philosophizing in both the Anglo-Saxon and francophone worlds, whether it be under the standard of Feyerabend's 'epistemological anarchism', Derrida's 'deconstruction', or

Foucault's 'power-knowledge'. Elsewhere I have defended realism against the post-structuralist attacks at more length than I can spare here.[16] Richard Rorty, in his important recent book *Philosophy and the Mirror of Nature* (1980), has argued, in a manner that echoes Deleuze, Derrida, and Foucault, that realism, and indeed the bulk of post-Cartesian philosophy, is based on the concept of *representation*: 'To know is to represent accurately what is outside the mind; to understand the possibility and nature of knowledge is to understand the way in which the mind is able to construct such representations. Philosophy's general concern is to be a general theory of representation.'[17] Rorty argues that recent developments in analytical philosophy have undermined the notion of the mind as the mirror of nature, and it is clear that he believes that realism is implicated in the general collapse of the representational view.

To understand more clearly what Rorty is getting at, let us consider W. V. O. Quine's celebrated 'Two Dogmas of Empiricism' (1951). The dogmas under examination are, first, 'a belief in some fundamental cleavage between truths which are *analytic*, or grounded in meanings independently of matters of fact, and truths which are *synthetic*, or grounded in fact', and, second, 'the belief that each meaningful statement is equivalent to some logical construct upon terms which refer to immediate experience'.[18] Much of Quine's article is devoted to demolishing Kant's distinction between analytic and synthetic judgements, on the basis of an attack on the very concept of meaning itself, in so far as it is conceived as an occult mental property existing independently of speakers' dispositions to assent to or dissent from sentences. The effect is to undermine a certain picture of language, most clearly expounded by the logical positivists (the immediate target of Quine's criticisms), but in some form shared very widely, in which the meanings of our words are first fixed, and then we use these words to state our beliefs about the world. Analytic truths express the rules of our language, which are independent of the specific structure of reality but enable us to make synthetic judgements concerning this reality. Quine is trying to show that one cannot separate questions of meaning and matters of fact in this manner: they are determined simultaneously. He expressed this in a famous image: 'The lore of our fathers is a fabric of sentences. . . . It is a pale grey lore, black with fact and white with convention. But I have found no substantial reason for concluding that there are any quite black threads in it, or any white ones.'[19] The conventions which determine the senses of expressions, and which analytic truths supposedly express, are not established independently of our assent to the sentences which state our beliefs.

Quine's refusal to distinguish sharply between questions of linguistic meaning and matters of empirical fact leads on to his rejection of the second dogma, whose core is the notion that the sense of every expression is determined independently of that of other expressions. But, as Davidson puts it, 'if meaning and belief are interlocked, then the idea that each belief has a definite object, and the idea that each word and sentence has a definite meaning, cannot be invoked in describing the goal of a successful theory [of meaning]'.[20] Quine puts it in the following terms. The Vienna Circle believed that the sense of a sentence is given by its conditions of verification, in other words, by the evidence which would establish its truth or falsity. But, as Pierre Duhem pointed out, experiments do not corroborate or refute single sentences, but great blocks of theory:

> The physicist can never subject an isolated hypothesis to experimental test, but only a whole group of hypotheses; when the experiment is in disagreement with his predictions, what he learns is that at least one of the hypotheses constituting this group is unacceptable and ought to be modified.[21]

It is always open to the scientist to reject, not the theory from which he inferred the falsified hypothesis, but rather, for example, the background observational theory in terms of which he interpreted the experimental results. Indeed, Duhem argues that 'the only experimental check on a physical theory which is not illogical consists in comparing *the entire system of the physical theory with the whole group of experimental laws*'.[22] Quine concludes that the senses of sentences are determined, not singly, but collectively, through their shared relation to sense-experience. 'The unit of empirical significance is the whole of science', which is 'like a field of force whose boundary conditions are experience'.[23]

This picture of language as a 'fabric of sentences', in which questions of meaning and of fact are so interwoven that the sense of any given sentence depends on its connection with all the other sentences, draws out a feature of post-Fregean philosophy, its anti-atomism. The sense of an expression is not given by its relation to some extra-linguistic entity, whether it be a subjective experience or an objective state of affairs, but is determined by its place in the network of sentences. Michael Dummett, although highly critical of many aspects of Quine's philosophy of language, concedes that 'Frege's model is similar in general structure' to 'the image which Quine presents . . . of language as an articulated structure which makes contact with reality, or with our experience of reality, only at the periphery'.[24] This model is separable from some of Quine's more questionable presumptions, his behaviourism and physicalism, and from some of his more controversial theses, such as the indeterminacy of radical translation. It is strikingly similar in outline to Saussure's account of language, which provides post-structuralist philosophers of language with one important starting point. As Frederic Jameson puts it, 'the philosophical conception behind [Saussurian linguistics] . . . is that it is not so much the individual word or sentence that "stands for" or "reflects" the individual object or event in the real world, but rather that the entire system of signs, the entire field of *langue*, lies parallel to reality itself.'[25]

Surely this model, whether Fregean or Saussurian, spells disaster to any attempt to treat language, or thought (for the two are inseparable), as a representation or reflection of reality. As Rorty puts it, if we 'think of knowledge as a relation to propositions, and thus of justification as a relation between the propositions in question and other propositions from which the former may be inferred . . ., we will see no need to end the potentially infinite regress of propositions-brought-forward-in-defence-of-other-propositions'.[26] Our discourse about the world can have no secure resting point in the world itself. The point can be sharpened by returning to 'Two Dogmas'. Quine argues that the report of an observation inconsistent with the sentences we hold to be true refutes no individual sentence, but merely requires some alteration in the totality of these sentences. We may, if we so wish, eliminate the inconvenient basic statement by, for example, altering the observational theory on which its interpretation depends, if we are prepared to take the trouble that revising probably quite a large number of sentences will involve. Equally, if no isolated sentence may be verified or falsified by observation, no sentence, even a logical law, is immune from revision. The effect of this argument is to undermine the notion of 'epistemological objectivity' introduced at the beginning of this section. If Quine is right, then it would seem that there are no objective standards which permit us to determine the truth or falsity of a theory. We may always, in the face of a recalcitrant experience, adopt what Popper called 'conventionalist stratagems', saving our theory by making adjustments elsewhere in our conceptual scheme. Our choice of which sentences to hold true will be guided by considerations of simplicity, elegance, or utility, criteria which are essentially subjective, offering no guidance concerning the truth or falsity of our beliefs.

We might put the point in Hegelian terms by saying that there is no immediate knowledge. Since Descartes, philosophy has sought to give our knowledge a secure foundation by tracing it to the subject's direct acquaintance with its object. Rorty suggests that this approach has its source in the assimilation, dating back to Plato and Aristotle, of knowledge to perception, so that we can only be said to know something when the object of knowledge is directly present to our consciousness. On this account, 'knowledge that' some proposition *p* is the case is parasitic upon 'knowledge of' some object, idea, impression *a* represented by *p* (or, better, by some word composing *p*).[27] But once we understand that knowledge, 'the lore of our fathers', is propositional, 'a fabric of sentences', then such an attempt to base it upon the presence of *a* to consciousness collapses. Hegel, even though, like Frege after him, he treated language as merely the inessential garb of thought, took this point when he rejected Schelling's and Jacobi's attempts to found speculative knowledge on an immediate intuition of the Absolute. He treated knowledge as irreducibly conceptual and sought to show how the most simple and indeterminate of concepts, Being, could generate, through a process every step of which could be rationally justified, an articulated system of concepts whose internal structure constituted the attainment of self-consciousness by the Absolute.

It is interesting that Adorno should pose the problem of a Marxist appropriation of Hegel in very similar terms. The assumption of 'the identity of subject and object', he wrote, 'enabled Hegel to conceal the antagonistic demands of observation and interpretation' (see Chapter 3, Section 3 above). The denial of immediate knowledge did not entail for Hegel the impossibility of 'epistemological objectivity', since every proposition finds a certain degree of truth, and ultimate justification, as one step in the self-realization of Spirit. But remove the Absolute, and the entire, elaborate structure collapses. The problem is an especially acute one because Marx in the *Grundrisse* and *Capital*, and Lenin in the *Philosophical Notebooks*, endorsed a conception of science as an articulated system of concepts, 'rising from the abstract to the concrete', derived directly from Hegel. But, once we recognize that knowledge is propositional – that, as Popper put it, '*statements can be justified only by statements*'[28] – can we hope to say of any theoretical discourse anything more than the sociological remark that some people hold it to be true? The Marxist philosopher to have most clearly grasped that immediate knowledge is impossible, Althusser, responded to this challenge by treating theoretical discourses as closed systems immune from empirical confirmation or refutation, and denying the existence of any general criteria by which to evaluate them.[29]

Imre Lakatos has, in my view, shown convincingly that there are standards which permit us to appraise the relative merit of scientific theories. The history of the sciences is characterized, he argued, by the existence of series of theories forming scientific research programmes. Each programme 'consists of methodological rules: some tell us what paths of research to avoid (*negative heuristic*), and others what paths to pursue.'[30] The latter rules form the 'positive heuristic', which 'consists of a partially articulated set of suggestions or hints on how to change, to develop the "refutable variants" of the research-programme'.[31] The heuristic forms an irrefutable 'hard core' of the programme, which is treated as immune from falsification; around it forms a 'protective belt' of falsifiable 'auxiliary hypotheses'. The programme develops by modifying, or adding to these hypotheses in accordance with the heuristic, and in partial response to the confirmation or refutation of theories by observation. Any such adjustment in the 'protective belt' counts as progress if it meets these three criteria: (1) the new theory has excess empirical content, i.e. it predicts some novel fact (theoretical progress); (2) some of this content is corroborated by observation (empirical progress); (3) the hypothesis is consistent with the heuristic. A theory which does not meet these standards represents, in the case of (1) and (2) respectively, theoretical and empirical degeneration. The merit of this approach is that, like Quine's, it treats *all* sentences as revisable. A report of some observation incompatible with the current state of our knowledge may be rejected, provided that the resulting change meets Lakatos's three requirements. Should this new theory in turn be refuted by observation, then it is always permissible to explain its refutation away, although if this too lacks empirical support the suspicion will arise that we are dealing with a degenerating research programme. The important point is that at every stage the process is subject to objective controls. Any attempt to challenge the outcome of the application of Lakatos's criteria to a research programme must itself respect these criteria.

The significance of Lakatos's methodology of scientific research programmes lies in the way in which it combines respect for the anti-atomism of post-Fregean philosophy of language ('one cannot prove statements from experiences . . . *all* propositions of science are theoretical and, incurably, fallible')[32] with a highly sophisticated means of determining the relative merit of theories by virtue of their success in explaining the world. But there is more to it than that. Although Ian Hacking has recently claimed that '*Lakatos's problem is to provide a theory of objectivity without a representational theory of truth*',[33] it seems to me that Lakatos's methodology both requires, and lends support to a view of thought as, if not a representation of specific items of reality, then a reflection of the external world. Lakatos needs such a realist account of knowledge because it would provide a rationale for the whole attempt to give criteria by means of which to appraise our theories. If knowledge is indeed, as Rorty suggests, a conversation, to which the notion of the correspondence or non-correspondence of our sentences to the world has as little relevance as it does to discussions of aesthetic or political preference,[34] then what earthly point is there in trying to formulate objective standards which will permit us to say that one theory constitutes progress over another? (He continues none the less to talk about 'our best theory about things in general', whatever that may be.) It is only from the standpoint of our sentences' truth or falsity, which depends not on our preferences but the state of the world, that a methodology such as Lakatos's makes any sense.

This amounts to saying that 'epistemological' and 'semantico-ontological objectivity' hang together. A claim that a given hypothesis represents progress over some earlier version of a research programme or over a rival programme amounts to the statement that it is closer to the truth than its predecessor or competitor. Not that it is true, for two reasons. First, as we saw at the beginning of this chapter, a realist conception of truth requires that even the best corroborated hypothesis may be false. Secondly, if truth is the correspondence of reality and thought, then we could only conclusively establish the truth of a sentence by comparing discourse and the world, which presumes the existence of some Archimedean point outside discourse, which is, once we have rejected the notion of immediate knowledge, impossible. At the same time, Lakatos's methodology provides realism with much needed support, because it shows that we can accept the picture of language as an articulated system shared by Frege, Saussure, and Quine, and at the same time possess objective standards by means of which to appraise adjustments made in the 'fabric of sentences'. It is true that the image of the mind as the mirror of nature, and of language as representation does not survive the abandonment of the concept of immediate knowledge. Truth no longer involves the notion of thought as the image of reality; rather, it acts as a regulative principle, providing a standard by which to appraise our sentences. Papineau has called this a 'holist realism'.[35] Let us accept this description, but let us also note that it throws a new light onto Lenin's first philosophical intervention, so often derided by professional philosophers. The conception of knowledge as a process of infinite approximation to the truth advanced in *Materialism and Empirio-Criticism* has been vindicated by the work of the most advanced modern philosopher of science, Imre Lakatos.[36]

6. Language and Ideology

(1) The Poverty of Ideology

One of the characteristic features of Western Marxism is the attention given to ideology. By 'ideology' I mean what Marx called 'the legal, political, religious, artistic or philosophic – in short, ideological forms in which men become conscious of this conflict [i.e. that between the forces and relations of production] and fight it out'.[1] The extent of Western Marxism's interest can be gathered from such works of the Frankfurt school as *Studien über Authorität und Familie* (1936), the section of *Dialectic of Enlightenment* called 'Elements of Anti-Semitism' (1947), and the great collective study presided over by Adorno, *The Authoritarian Personality* (1950). All of these reflect, as Martin Jay puts it, a concern with 'the psychosocial mechanisms of obedience and sources of violence'.[2] Similarly, Althusser in his celebrated essay, 'Ideology and the Ideological State Apparatuses' (1970), sought to examine the ways in which bourgeois social relations are reproduced through ideology's ability to shape, and indeed to preform the conscious desires and beliefs of individuals. And Habermas's recent work has concentrated on the 'normative structures', law, morality, world-views, and the formation of individual and collective identities, whose development, he claims, is 'the pacemaker of social evolution'.[3]

This preoccupation with ideology has fairly obvious political sources. A shift towards consideration of the superstructural conditions of social stability and transformation was implicit in Lenin's rejection of the notion that workers automatically gravitate towards revolutionary consciousness. Once the overthrow of capitalism was no longer thought to be guaranteed by the workings of the economy, then the mechanisms supporting or undermining the capitalist order became the object of theoretical analysis. Thus, we find a stress on ideology in the revolutionary Hegelianism of the 1920s. Korsch wrote: 'The material relations of production of the capitalist epoch only are

127

what they are in combination with the forms in which they are reflected in the pre-scientific and bourgeois-scientific consciousness of the period; and they could not subsist in reality without these forms of consciousness'.[4] We saw in Chapter 3 how Lukács's attempt to marry Marxism and anti-naturalism led him to identify the achievement of self-consciousness by the proletariat, the absolute subject-object, with the overthrow of capitalism. Most important of all, of course, was Gramsci's distinction between force and consent: 'The supremacy of a social group manifests itself in two ways, as "domination" [i.e. coercive rule] and as "intellectual and moral leadership". . . . A social group can, and indeed must, already exercise "leadership" before winning governmental power (this indeed is one of the principal conditions of winning such power).'[5] This emphasis on the ideological conditions of proletarian revolution has been taken in recent years by the theoreticians of Eurocommunism to mean that the attainment of ideological 'hegemony' by the socialist movement is equivalent to the capture of political power.[6]

The enormous attention paid to ideology by Marxist theoreticians over the past 50 years must be set alongside the fact that there is no satisfactory account of ideology in Marx. His discussions of the subject involve two distinct, and conflicting elements. The first is what I have called elsewhere an *epistemological* conception of ideology.[7] Here ideology is conceived as a set of false beliefs, constituted by a dual relation, first, to the reality of which it is an inverted reflection, and, secondly, to the true, scientific knowledge of that reality. This conception of ideology is to be found in the work of the more radical *philosophes*: organized religion is a set of lies invented by a conspiratorial minority, the priests, despots, etc., in order to baffle the masses and keep them in thrall. The obverse, of course, is that another minority, this time an enlightened one armed with the truth, can free the masses from these deceptions by the power of reason alone. Feuerbach went much further, attempting a structural analysis of Christianity, and trying to show that it involved an inversion of subject and predicate, the transposition of man's species-being onto an alien and fictional entity. He also sought to make human self-estrangement more than the result of a plot to hoodwink the ruled, explaining it as a historically necessary phase in the formation of self-consciousness. Marx took over the model of inversion (*Verkehrung*), but sought to show that its presence in consciousness is merely the reflection of an inverted reality. 'If in ideology men and their relations appear upside-down as in a *camera obscura*, this phenomenon arises just as much from their historical life-process as the inversion of objects on the retina does from their physical life-process.' (*CW* 5:36.) There is, however, a second, 'pragmatic' dimension to Marx's conception of ideology: the illusions generated by the 'historical life-process' serve the interests of the ruling class by smoothing over and concealing the contradictions of class society. They do so because 'the ideas of the ruling class are in every epoch the ruling ideas' (ibid., 59). But this statement is justified in terms that have nothing to do with the truth or falsity of ideological discourse, but rather concern the institutionalization of class power: 'the class which has the material means of production at its disposal, consequently also controls the means of mental production, so that the ideas of those that lack the means of mental production are on the whole subject to them.' (Ibid.)

It may seem that there is no tension between the two dimensions of Marx's concept of ideology, that the 'pragmatic' element merely gives historical specificity to the epistemological, showing how 'false consciousness' takes shape as the product of an inverted reality through an account of what Göran Therborn calls the material determination of ideologies. Some of the tensions between the two aspects of ideology can be brought out by considering Marx's only detailed attempt to give such an account, in his analysis of commodity fetishism in *Capital*. This account is closely connected to the labour theory of value.[8] Marx argued that capitalism, as a system of generalized commodity production, necessarily involves the division of the economy into a set of competing capitals. In these circumstances, the concrete, useful labours performed to produce particular use-values count as social labour, part of the total activity carried out to meet the needs of society, through the exchange of their products on the market. The effect is to transform these specific productive activities into quantities of abstract social labour, expressed in the values of commodities as the socially necessary labour-time required to produce them. Furthermore, the essentially social activity of production takes on the form of a process governed by the movements of commodities in the market. 'the definite social relation between men themselves . . . assumes here, for them, the fantastic form of a relation between things.' (*C* i. 165.) Capitalist social relations are thus naturalized: in the most extreme case of commodity fetishism, the trinity formula, the incomes of landowners, workers, and capitalists are determined by the technical contribution to the production of use-values made by the 'factors of production' they represent, land, labour and capital, so that historically specific relations of production are transformed into essential features of any labour process.

Marx made three important points about commodity fetishism. First the fetishized forms of capitalist relations of production are the mode of appearance of these relations, 'the form which they assume in the surface of society, in the action of different capitals upon one another, in competition, and in the ordinary conscious-ness of the agents of production themselves' (C iii. 25). Secondly, this form of appearance is not pure illusion; it has a real basis which arises from the functioning of capitals in the process of competition. 'To the producers,' Marx stresses, 'the social relations between their private labours appear as *what they are*, i.e. they do not appear as direct social relations between people, but rather as material relations between people and social relations between things.' (C i. 166; italics added.) Even the trinity formula has a certain measure of truth, since, without the division of newly created value into wages, profit, and rent, the reproduc-tion of social classes would be impossible: 'This illusion would necessarily arise, because in the actual movement of individual capitals, and the commodities produced by them, . . . the compo-nents into which it [value] is split functions as a precondition of the value of the commodities.' (C iii. 870.) Thirdly, capitalist relations of production *generate* these illusions in its agents.

> These ready-made relations and forms [i.e. the division of new value into wages, profit, and rent], which appear as preconditions in real production . . ., confront it equally as ready-made preconditions in the process of reproduction. As such, they in fact determine the actions of individual capitalists, etc., and provide the motives which are reflected in their consciousness. Vulgar political economy does nothing more than express in doctrinaire fashion this consciousness, which, in respect of its motives and notions, remains in thrall to the appearance of the capitalist mode of production. (TSV iii. 485.)

It is on the first and the third of these propositions that I wish to concentrate, fetishism as the necessary form of appearance of capitalism induced in the consciousness of the agents of production by the process of competition. They are closely connected to the distinction between essence and appearance so important to Marx's conception of science, and they provide the basis for his counterposition of classical and vulgar political economy, the former penetrating beneath the surface, the latter merely systematizing the appearances. They are, however, profoundly problematic. Jacques Rancière explicates Marx's account of the formation of ideology in *Capital* as follows: 'The place of the agents of production in the process determines . . . the necessary representations of their practice as simple expressions of the apparent movement of capital and thus as totally inverted by relation to its real movement.'[9] The structure of capitalism thus produces its own misperception. This analysis presumes the possibility of immediate knowledge: the agent of production, once placed within capitalist relations of production, will perceive reality in a certain way, purely by virtue of the position he or she occupies. There is no room for conceptualization, for the interpretation of experience, in the formation of 'the ordinary consciousness of the agents of production themselves'. The appearances will admit of only one interpretation – a false interpretation as it happens, but this will become clear only if we penetrate beneath the surface.[10]

This account of how ideology is formed must, it seems to me, be rejected. This is partly for philosophical reasons. The considerations adduced in Chapter 5 weigh heavily against the possibility of immediate knowledge. Experience is always already conceptualized; no perception admits of only one interpretation. In Quinean terms, we can always reinterpret a recalcitrant experience by making the necessary adjustments in our conceptual scheme. Even our acquaintance with the capitalist system at the most everyday level involves some conceptualization. Vulgar economy (and its neo-classical heirs) is, like *Capital*, a theorization of a reality which admits of no unique interpretation, and is to be judged, like *Capital*, by its relative degree of success in interpreting the observable, but always reinterpretable behaviour of capitalism. There are also political reasons for rejecting the theory of fetishism. For the claim that capitalist relations of production generate their own ideological misrecognition automatically, merely by virtue of their daily functioning, suggests that capitalism can reproduce itself indefinitely, lending support to a pessimistic version of Kautskyian evolutionism. It also precludes empirical enquiry into the formation of ideologies, since the theory of fetishism presents us with the spontaneous generation of false consciousness. No great damage would be done to *Capital* by the excision of commodity fetishism: as I have shown elsewhere it is an error to believe that the essence/appearance contrast is the organizing figure of Marx's discourse.[11] The rational kernel of the theory, the proposition that capitalism functions through the competition of capitals and the circulation of their products, is salvageable; it is, in any case, evidently true that capitalism involves the rule of men by their products, as every economic crisis shows us.

It is easy to understand Marx's error when we consider the origins of his conception of ideology. He took over the notion of the inversion of subject and predicate which Feuerbach regarded as characteristic of both the Hegelian dialectic and religion, and placed the site of this inversion in social reality. The image of a 'topsy turvy world' ('*auf den Kopf gestellte Welt*') is to be found in Marx's writings from his 1843 correspondence with Arnold Ruge to *Capital* Volume iii. (See *CW* 3:139, *C* iii. 830.) The notion of inversion was transferred by Marx from the critique of religion and philosophy to that of politics and political economy.[12] This process is closely related to Marx's setting of Hegel onto his feet. For example, in the appendix to the first (1867) edition of *Capital* Volume i, Marx discussed how the exchange of commodities reduced concrete, useful labours to abstract social labour, commenting:

> This *inversion* by which the sensibly-concrete counts only as the form of appearance of the abstractly general, and not, on the contrary, the abstractly general as property of the concrete, characterizes the expression of value. At the same time, it makes understanding it difficult. If I say: Roman Law and German Law are both laws, that is obvious. But if I say: Law, this abstraction, *realizes itself* in Roman Law and in German Law, in these concrete laws, the interconnection becomes mystical.[13]

As Rancière points out, 'the process which characterizes the mode of existence of value here is that which for the young Marx characterized the operation of Hegelian speculation, such as he illustrates in *The Holy Family* by the dialectic of the abstract Fruit realizing itself in concrete pears and almonds.'[14] We saw in Chapter 2 that Marx tended to conceive value as a Hegelian concrete universal. But there is a problem in merely asserting that 'reality is itself speculative' for Marx, that capitalism possesses the properties of the Absolute Idea. This is not simply the general problem of Hegel's teleological dialectic; for Being, as the immediate unity of subject and object has the capacity to generate its own self-consciousness. This occurs in the sphere of Essence, where Being is 'intro-reflected', conscious of itself as divided into essence and appearance. Marx's inversion of Hegel has the effect of endowing capitalist relations of production with the ability to reflect upon themselves, in the form of fetishism. As Adorno puts it, 'the fetish character of the commodity . . . is dialectical, in the eminent sense that it produces consciousness.'[15] The theory of fetishism is one of the privileged points at which we encounter the persistence of Hegelian categories in *Capital.*

The Lukácian theory of reification solves the conceptual difficulties of the theory of fetishism, at the price of identifying social relations with forms of consciousness. There is then no problem about the material determination of ideologies, since ideology is the stuff of social life. Precisely for this reason, Adorno came to distance himself from the concept of reification: 'centering theory around reification, a form of consciousness, makes the critical theory idealistically acceptable to the reigning consciousness and to the collective unconscious.' (*ND* 190.) However, as we have seen, he attached great importance to the notion of commodity fetishism, treating the Hegelian Absolute as the reflection of the 'topsy turvy world' in which concrete labours are transformed into abstract social labour: 'Hegel's transposition of the particular into particularity [i.e. into a concept] follows the practice of a society that tolerates the particular only as a category, a form of the supremacy of the universal.' (Ibid., 334.)[16] Moreover, he continued to treat the social formation as an expressive totality whose essence is reflected at all its levels. However formally valid Adorno's criticisms of Benjamin's *Passagenarbeit*, for example, his comment that 'the theological motif of calling things by their names tends to turn into a wide-eyed presentation of mere facts',[17] Benjamin's attempt to grasp cultural phenomena in their singularity seems to carry more promise than the Hegelian-Marxist alternative. What Susan Buck-Morss calls Adorno's 'effort . . . to discover the truth of the social totality . . . as it quite literally *appeared* within the object in a particular configuration'[18] treats the relation of whole and parts, economy and ideology, as quite unproblematic, the reflection of the former in the latter. Benjamin, on the other hand, by starting from the specificity of objects, permits us to conceptualize social phenomena in their complex and differential relations of determination.[19]

More generally, Marxist theories of ideology have tended to assume, without proof, that it is through ideology that social formations are reproduced. Indeed, the role of cultural and symbolic practices tends to be explained simply by their contribution to perpetuating the dominant relations of production. The functionalist overtones of such an approach are evident in Althusser's claim that '*ideology (as a system of mass representations) is indispensable in any society if men are to be formed, transformed and equipped to respond to the demands of their conditions of existence*' (FM 235). This is very close to the traditional sociological conception of normative structures as the cement of social life. Not only does such an approach tend to discourage analysis of the material determination of ideologies; by its presumption that ideology is functional to ruling-class hegemony, Gramsci's 'moral and intellectual leadership', it precludes empirical enquiry into the actual role played by ideologies in definite social formations. It is striking to see how both Frankfurt and Althusserian Marxism share a common view of the working class as automatons unable to escape the maw of the 'culture industry' or the 'ideological state apparatuses'. One recent study has drawn on historical evidence to challenge the proposition that 'the ideas of the ruling class are in every epoch the ruling ideas', arguing that the ruling ideology has served mainly to unify the dominant class, while the masses have been controlled by the cruder mechanisms of physical coercion and economic incentives and disincentives.[20] These claims, if true, undercut completely the tendency of Western Marxists to attribute magical properties to bourgeois ideology.

Over and above such empirical questions, it seems to me that further progress in the Marxist theory of ideology requires two steps, both advocated by Göran Therborn in his interesting book *The Ideology of Power and the Power of Ideology* (1980). They can be summed up as the rejection of the conception of ideology as 'false consciousness'. This implies, first, scrapping the epistemological element of Marx's theory of ideology, a conception which is at work in the theory of fetishism, encouraging the view of capitalism as a system which generates its own false interpretation. If we take seriously the 'pragmatic' dimension of ideology, the determination of ideologies by the class struggle, then the question of the truth or falsity of ideologies is beside the point. What matters is that they are the 'forms in which men become conscious of this conflict and fight it out'. Althusser wrote that ideology is a representation of 'the *lived* relation between men and their world', and went on to say that this was an 'imaginary' relation (*FM* 233). What I propose is that we dispense with the notion that ideologies are *imaginary* representations, false beliefs, illusions; ideology is, on Therborn's definition, 'that aspect of the human condition under which human beings live their lives as conscious actors in a world that makes sense to them to various degrees'.[21] Secondly, if ideology is not false, then neither is it consciousness. To quote Althusser again, 'ideology is indeed a system of representations, but in the majority of cases these have nothing to do with "consciousness": they are usually images and occasionally concepts, but it is above all as *structures* that they impose on the vast majority of men.' (*FM* 233.) More precisely, ideologies are practices which function symbolically, usually through the generation of utterances, subject to definite norms and constraints. Very often these norms and constraints derive from the prevailing structure of class power.[22]

Neither of these proposals implies that we must reject the distinction between science and ideology, rather that we must conceive of it in a different way than *Capital* or *Reading Capital* does. Theoretical discourse is characterized by the formation of scientific research programmes, which are relatively autonomous, functioning through the construction of hypotheses in accordance with the guidelines laid down by the programme's heuristic. Ideologies differ from the sciences not in representing raw, unconceptualized experience (which does not exist), but in their lack of this relative autonomy, their existence within relations of power, which circumscribe the possible utterances within a given ideological discourse. Research programmes, although powered internally by their heuristic, generally emerge from ideologies in specific historical conditions, and very often continue to function in close connection with them. One can, therefore, both treat neo-classical economics as a scientific research programme – evaluating it in accordance with Lakatos's three criteria – and analyse its intimate relation to neo-liberal ideology. Marxism, of course, differs from other theoretical discourses in disdaining to conceal its 'ideological' connotations.

(2) Two Concepts of Language

One implication of the argument of the previous section is to push Marxism in the direction of the philosophy of language. The move is, in any case, a logical one. For, once we accept that thought and language are interdependent, then the study of ideologies must involve an analysis of the systems of signs through which they are expressed. And such analysis presupposes some general account of how signification itself occurs, in other words, what analytical philosophers would call a theory of meaning. The first major encounter between Marxism and the philosophy of language occurred in the 1920s, in the work of the Russian formalists, and of Mikhail Bakhtin. The latter acknowledged that in attempting to formulate a Marxist account of language he was starting from scratch.[23] Of more recent importance has been the attempt by the Parisian Marxism of the 1960s and 1970s (Althusser and his followers, the *Tel Quel* group during their *marxisant* phase) to appropriate the philosophy of language stemming from Saussure and considerably developed by Lévi-Strauss, Jakobson, and Lacan. I have already suggested in Chapter 5 one major similarity between the Saussurian conception of language and the Fregean one broadly accepted by analytical philosophers. For both, the senses of expressions are determined, not by their relation to the extra-linguistic objects to which they refer, but by their place within the network of language itself.

The immanence of meaning in language has a number of important consequences. First, it implies that sense is a *surface* phenomenon, as Gilles Deleuze has forcefully argued from within the Saussurian tradition.[24] In other words, to account for the process through which expressions acquire a meaning does not involve postulating the existence of some more fundamental, extra-linguistic level of reality which explains this process. The sense and reference of expressions are determined by the position they occupy within the network of language: there is no need to invoke their referents, or some psychological or psycho-social mechanism from which the interrelations of sentences are supposed to derive (although, of course, such a mechanism may be necessary to account for our possession of the *capacity* to use language: what is at issue here is merely whether this mechanism is needed to explain what we do when we exercise this capacity). Wittgenstein seems very close to Deleuze in the following passages. 'The problems arising through a misinterpretation of our forms of language have the character of *depth*,' he wrote.

> This finds expression in questions as to the *essence* of language, of propositions, of thought. – For if we too in these investigations are trying to understand the essence of language – its function, its structure, – Yet *this* is not what those questions have in view. For they see in the essence, not something that already lies open to view and that becomes surveyable by a rearrangement, but something that lies *beneath* the surface.[25]

The essence of language is a phenomenon of the surface because it is to be ascertained, not by discovering some 'foundation' outside language, but within the 'fabric of sentences' itself.

There is another important overlap between Fregean and Saussurian conceptions of language, one to which I have already adverted in Chapter 1, namely, the denial of a constitutive role to the subject. The function of synthesis which Kant held to depend on the activity of a transcendental subject was made by Frege immanent in language, requiring no further explanation: the meanings of words derives from their role in sentences, and the latter's relations are to be analysed without reference to any transcendental presuppositions of experience, and without consideration of the psychological processes which accompany a particular assertion or inference.[26] Popper developed the implications of this approach most explicitly when he conceptualized knowledge, not as true beliefs, the property of individual subjects, but as the 'third world', distinct from both physical objects and mental processes and constituted by the objective relations subsisting between sentences.[27] As Ian Hacking points out, this extreme anti-psychologism is not unique to Popper or his followers, such as Lakatos; it is present in Quine's treatment of the 'lore of our fathers' as a 'fabric of sentences', and in Althusser's conception of 'theoretical practice' as a 'process without a subject'.[28] It is, in a sense, implicit in the anti-atomism characteristic of both French and analytical philosophers, although one should note the Kantian themes raised by some of the latter, for example, by P. F. Strawson in his attempts to establish the necessary features of any conceptual scheme that will permit the identification of particulars.

There is, however, one fundamental difference between Fregean and Saussurian accounts of language. While analytical philosophy treats the sentence as primary in explaining the workings of language, structural linguistics and its philosophical heirs make no distinction of principle between words and sentences, concentrating instead on the selection and combination of linguistic units, which may be phonemes, words, sentences, or even larger segments of discourse. The significance of this difference becomes clear when we consider what, since Chomsky, has become known as *linguistic creativity*, the capacity of speakers to understand, and construct sentences which they have never before uttered, heard, read, or imagined. Clearly any theory of meaning must provide an explanation of this phenomenon of the openness of language.[29] The broad approach taken by anyone accepting a post-Fregean philosophy of language to this problem is quite straightforward. We possess a stock of words which acquire a sense and a reference only in the context of a sentence, but which exist as our vocabulary independent of their use on any occasion. We are able to understand and construct new sentences because each sentence is a permutation of words with which we are already acquainted. The distinction between words and sentences is, therefore, crucial in accounting for linguistic creativity. Because of their failure to make such a distinction, post-Saussurian philosophers of language tend to argue that every new utterance involves the introduction of new meanings into the language. Thus, when we use a word with which we are already acquainted in uttering a novel sentence, then we are assigning a new sense to this word, in effect, creating a new word. It is only thus that we can explain Jacques Lacan's claim that communication necessarily involves misunderstanding.[30] Any attempt to communicate with another person is inherently ambiguous because conveying some new thought involves a sleight-of-hand in which words acquire different meanings. Language in use continually pulls the rug away from under itself. Post-structuralist philosophers are led to introduce such concepts as 'lack', 'absence', 'empty space', 'floating signifier', 'sliding' in order to account for the phenomenon of signification because for them it is a process in which the senses of expressions can never be grasped without one being referred to a new sense.

The point can be sharpened by comparing the very different accounts of metaphor given by Fregean and Saussurian theories of language. Analytical philosophers tend to regard the metaphorical meanings of expressions as parasitic upon their literal meanings. An extreme version of this approach is Donald Davidson's, where a metaphor has no meaning other than its literal meaning: what leads us to ascribe to it a separate, metaphorical meaning is the *effect* of such a sentence as 'The moon's a balloon', whose sense, like that of any other sentence, is determined by the normal sense of its component words, and which is, like most metaphors, false (the moon isn't a balloon), but which 'makes us attend to some likeness, often a novel or surprising likeness, between two things'.[31] Lacan, by contrast, treats metaphor and metonymy, respectively the substitution of expressions for one another and their combination, as constitutive of language.[32] Thus, the ambiguities which critics such as William Empson have held to be characteristic of many poetic effects turn out to be essential to signification itself. The result is what Frederic Jameson calls 'the incommensurability of language, the fact that language cannot express any *thing*: only relationships (Saussurian linguistics) or sheer absence (Mallarmé)'.[33] There can be no resting point in language thus conceptualized: every attempt to say something new must subvert the apparently stable meanings that expressions possess by virtue of their place within the network of language. No wonder that both Deleuze and Derrida have described language as *play*, a system of differences functioning through a potentially infinite process of metaphorical substitutions and metonymic combinations.[34]

The importance of this treatment of language is that it encourages a view of reality itself as difference, flux, fragments, a metaphysical position given its most coherent expression by Deleuze.[35] Such an approach can have serious epistemological and political consequences. For it implies that any attempt to stabilize the flux, to impose order on difference is reactionary. Consider Althusser's account of the distinction between science and ideology in terms of the opposition between openness and closure: the development of a science is potentially infinite, while an ideology merely presents predigested solutions to predetermined questions, constituting a mirror-structure which serves to provide support for extra-discursive religious, ethical, or political interests. (See *RC* 52, 90 n.) Leaving aside the vagueness of the contrast, let us note how dangerous its implications are. For *any* theoretical discourse – quantum mechanics, neo-classical economics, psychoanalysis, scholastic metaphysics – is closed in the sense of forbidding the utterance of certain statements. This is clear when we think of a Lakatosian research programme, whose heuristic both lays down the broad direction of research to be pursued, and forbids the acceptance of statements inconsistent with the programme's hard core.[36] Marxism is, in this sense, a closed discourse: it rules out certain forms of explanation, e.g. in terms of forms of consciousness or racial types, as incompatible with the primacy of production relations. Science may, as Althusser says (quoting Lenin), be infinite, but it does not follow that we are free to adopt or reject any sentence. The point can be made in more general terms. The principle of non-contradiction imposes a certain closure upon our discourse, by requiring us, if we accept certain sentences to reject others. (We are forbidden, in other words, to assert 'It is raining and it is not raining'.) Yet once we come to regard discourse as inherently unstable and ambiguous, then any attempt, however modest, to impose constraints on what may be asserted at any given time becomes a philosophical mistake. Indeed, Foucault and Deleuze in their recent, 'anarcho-Nietzschean' phase, have come to see the presence of closure within discourse as the index of the existence of 'power-knowledge', the formation and control of both thought and reality within relations of domination.[37]

While there were independent political and theoretical reasons for the adoption of such a position by a section of the French intelligentsia in the 1970s, undoubtedly one factor contributing to its formation was a philosophy of language which could account for linguistic creativity by denying to words a stable meaning. This seems to be a consideration in favour of a Fregean theory of language, in which the possibility of uttering or understanding an indefinite number of unfamiliar sentences is directly given in the proposition that words acquire a sense and reference from the role they play in the formation of sentences. (Such a view does not, of course, deny that words change their meaning over time; it is concerned with the simultaneous determination of the senses of expressions by their places within the language-game.) A conception of language along Fregean lines seems to offer the Marxist theory of ideology more than its Saussurian competitor.

(3) Truth and Communication

There is an obvious objection which some Marxists might make to the very notion of a systematic theory of meaning. It amounts to saying that the project of giving a general account of the way in which the sense and reference of expressions are determined is misconceived. Words and sentences acquire a meaning only in the specific context of their use, and this context cannot be separated from the non-discursive social practices with which discourse is interwoven. Such an objection is often taken to be implied in Wittgenstein's slogan, 'the meaning of a word is its use in the language'[38] (although this interpretation is by no means uncontroversial). Michael Dummett's reply to this objection seems to me conclusive:

> The fact that anyone who has a mastery of any given language is able to understand an infinity of sentences, an infinity which is, of course, principally composed of sentences which he has never heard before . . . can hardly be explained otherwise than by supposing that each speaker has an implicit grasp of a number of general principles governing the use in sentences of words of the language . . . It is hard to see how there can be any theoretical obstacle to making those principles explicit; and an explicit statement of those principles an implicit grasp of which constitutes mastery of the language would be, precisely, a complete theory of meaning for the language.[39]

To clarify the problem of the articulation of language on other social practices, we must first consider an important distinction drawn by Frege between the sense and force of sentences. The sense of a sentence is the thought it expresses, 'the part that alone can be accepted as true or rejected as false'.[40] However, 'we can express a thought without asserting it . . . Once we have grasped a thought, we can recognize it as true (*make a judgement*) and give expression to our recognition of its truth (*make an assertion*).'[41] A thought is asserted when the indicative sentence expressing it is uttered with assertoric force, and Frege devised a special sign, the judgement-stroke, to make the distinction between sense and force perspicuous in his logical notation.[42] Frege confined his discussion to assertoric sentences, which alone admit of truth or falsity – a command ('Close the door!') or a question ('Are you coming tonight?') is neither true or false. This restriction was natural enough, since Frege's interest was in logic, which deals with the transmission of truth and falsity between sentences, but the distinction can be generalized to cover other classes of utterances, a move made by J. L. Austin in his *How to Do Things with Words* (1962). On Dummett's version of this generalization, every type of utterance, or speech act, whether it be a question, command, assertion, promise, or whatever, has

> a certain descriptive content which is in general independent of whether it is being used to make an assertion or give a command; this descriptive content corresponds precisely to what Frege calls the sense of a sentence, or the thought it expresses. In order to understand the sentence, to know its use, it will be necessary that it should contain another symbolic element, conveying the force with which it is used; something playing the role of an assertion sign or a command sign . . . On this view, assertoric sentences, imperatives, sentential interrogatives, and optatives would all express thoughts: they would differ only in the force attaching to them – the linguistic act which is performed by uttering them.[43]

The distinction between sense and force is essential to understanding one of the main divisions between analytical philosophers of language. Strawson draws a contrast between the theorists of formal semantics, and the theorists of communication-intention.[44] The former, Davidson and his followers, take sense as primary, claiming that the meaning of a sentence is given by its truth-conditions, which are generally independent of the conditions of utterance. On the other hand, speech-act theorists, such as John Searle, argue that the meaning of expressions is determined by the force with which they are uttered, and which conveys the intentions of the speaker, either the actual intentions with which the utterance is made, or those conventionally associated with speech acts of that sort.

This latter approach to language, that of communication-intention, has been taken over by Jürgen Habermas in his recent attempts to construct a 'formal pragmatics' which will permit the conceptualization of the 'general presuppositions of communicative action'.[45] This project was prefigured in *Knowledge and Human Interests* (1968), a forceful restatement of anti-naturalism which sharply distinguished the structures of 'communicative action' (language and culture) from those of 'instrumental action' (the labour process, governed by the instrumental rationality oriented to selecting the most efficient means of controlling nature). Habermas's conclusion brought together Adorno's belief that language spontaneously overcomes the opposition between universal and particular with Fichte's notion of reason as inseparable from the striving for human emancipation: 'What raises us out of nature is the only thing whose nature we know: *language*. Through its structure, autonomy and responsibility are posited for us. Our first sentence expresses unequivocally the intention of universal and unrestrained consensus.' To the extent that it is only in an emancipated society that this intention can be realized, 'the truth of statements is based on anticipating the good life'.[46]

Habermas has sought to give substance to this claim by resort to Austin's and Searle's theory of speech acts, in the process abandoning some of the more strictly Kantian aspects of his earlier views: 'experiences are, if we follow the basic Kantian idea, constituted; utterances are at most generated.'[47] Every speech act, Habermas argues, involves certain validity claims, which express the speaker's intentions to be understood, to tell the truth, to do so sincerely, and in an appropriate manner. The objective of any speech-act is to come to an understanding, that is, 'to bring about an agreement that terminates in the intersubjective mutuality of reciprocal understanding, shared knowledge, mutual trust, and accord with one another'.[48] This structure is presupposed by the relations of production, which merely embody 'a specific form of social integration' that secures 'the unity of a social life-world' through the values and norms.[49] It is this form, or 'principle of organization', which determines a society's level of development, expressed in its learning capacity. (Habermas assimilates the evolution of society to that of individual agents.) Social evolution takes place 'in the form of the directional learning-processes that work through redeemable validity-claims' of the sort made in every speech-act.[50]

There is something profoundly ideological, in the pejorative sense of concealing contradictions, about a theoretical project which explicitly assumes that society is constituted by communication, that 'other forms of social action – for example, conflict, competence, strategic action in general – are derivates of action oriented to reaching understanding'.[51] The result is that opposition to human emancipation is *irrational*:

For a living being that maintains itself in the structure of ordinary-language communication, the validity-basis of speech has the binding force of universal and unavoidable – in this sense transcendental –

presupposition . . . If we are not free then to reject or accept the validity-claims bound up with the cognitive potential of the human species, it is senseless to want to 'decide' for or against reason, for or against the expansion of the potential of reasoned action.[52]

In the first place, it seems an unwarranted intrusion of Habermas's ethical and political views to define speech acts so as to exclude or render aberrant such typical forms of 'ordinary-language communication' as lies, threats, and racist jokes. Moreover, the belief that every member of society, whether Sir Michael Edwardes, a Yorkshire miner, or a British Movement skinhead, is committed by his or her utterances to the same goal of establishing 'universal and unrestrained consensus' drains out of historical materialism precisely what Marx had placed in the foreground – exploitation, antagonism, social conflict, class struggle. From a classical Marxist point of view, it is entirely rational for a capitalist to resist 'the expansion of the potential of reasoned action', for, by virtue of the position he occupies in the relations of production, it is not in his interest for these relations to be replaced by communist ones.

Habermas's definition of society as 'communicative action' is closely connected to his belief that Marx's conception of production reduces society to 'instrumental action', dedicated to the expansion of the productive forces. But, as I have tried to show in Chapters 2 and 4, Marx conceived of production as the articulated unity of the forces and relations of production, dismissing attempts 'to examine production while disregarding . . . [the] internal distribution' of the means of production which determines the specific form of appropriation of surplus-labour as 'an empty abstraction' (G 96). Habermas objects that 'the distribution inherent in production . . . is based on a structure of symbolic interaction . . . [which] cannot be analysed into elements of production, want, instrumental action and immediate consumption'.[53] Marx, of course, never argued that this distribution could be so analysed, carefully distinguishing it from the labour-process, the specific technical organization through which use-values are produced. But he regarded this distribution as constituted, not by 'symbolic interaction' or 'communicative action', but by the *antagonistic* forms in which direct producers and means of production are combined and separated in class societies, forms which are relations of exploitation and on whose basis the class struggle unfolds. Habermas's dissolution of this, the specific dimension of historical materialism, provides the justification for a reversion to left Hegelianism, conceiving human liberation as a process of education, the removal of the obstacles to the 'full understanding' that is the aspiration of every 'communicative action'.

There are, in any case, good reasons for rejecting any account of language in terms of communication-intention. There is, first, Dummett's objection to giving the meaning of expressions in terms of their specific conditions of utterance, namely, that it cannot account for the ability of the same words to figure in a potential infinity of sentences falling into many different classes of speech-act. In other words, the sense of an expression can be determined independently of the force with which it is uttered. A second important objection is made by Davidson:

> We cannot hope to attach a sense to the attribution of finely discriminated intentions independently of interpreting speech. The reason is not that we cannot ask necessary questions, but that interpreting an agent's intentions, his beliefs and his words are part of a single project, no part of which can be assumed to be complete before the rest is.[54]

This argument is closely related to Quine's attack, which we discussed in the last chapter, on accounts of language which separate questions of meaning from matters of fact, the process of assigning a sense and reference to expressions from the use of these expressions to state our beliefs. Indeed, what Michael Rosen calls the conventionalist account of meaning given by Habermas and other speech-act theorists makes precisely such a distinction: the meanings of expressions are determined by the implicit intersubjective agreement that is expressed in the rules governing speakers' linguistic practice.[55] This theory of language is open to challenge on the grounds that communication presupposes, rather than making possible, the existence of beliefs shared by all the interlocutors. This is one implication of Quine's argument that radical translation, the interpretation of another's utterances on the basis merely of his observed dispositions to assent to or dissent from sentences, will result in more than one correct version of the same sentences.[56] Interpretation is possible, Davidson argues, only on the basis of the 'principle of charity', according to which the other's beliefs, expressed in the sentences he holds true, will largely overlap with our own: 'If we cannot find a way to interpret the utterances and other behaviour of a creature as revealing a set of beliefs largely consistent and true by our own standards, we have no reason to count that creature as rational, as having beliefs, or as saying anything'.[57] Interestingly, Wittgenstein, usually claimed by communication-intention theorists as one of their own, expressed a very similar view:

> We say that, in order to communicate, people must agree with one another about the meanings of words. But the criterion for this agreement is not just agreement with reference to definitions, e.g., ostensive definitions – but *also* an agreement in judgements. It is essential for communication that we agree in a large number of judgements.[58]

Communication-intention theory is, in essence, a softened, socialized Kantianism, which substitutes for the transcendental subject an intersubjectivity whose tacit agreement on the rules of language renders communication possible. For Davidson, however, 'language is an instrument of communication because of its semantic dimension, the potentiality for truth or falsehood . . . of its utterances and inscriptions'.[59] The attraction of such an approach for anyone espousing the realism defended in the previous chapter should be obvious. Davidson's strategy is to build on the Fregean thesis that the sense of a sentence is given by its truth-conditions by extending Tarski's definition of truth in formalized languages to natural languages, thereby reading into the latter the conceptual apparatus of first-order logic.[60] Tarski's fundamental concept is that of satisfaction, the relationship between a predicate and the objects of which it is true, in terms of which the truth-conditions of whole sentences are then recursively defined. Davidson writes: 'the semantic concept of truth developed by Tarski deserves to be called a correspondence theory because of the part played by the concept of satisfaction; for clearly what has been done is that the property of being true has been explained, and non-trivially, in terms of a relation between language and something else.'[61] The application of these concepts to natural languages is intended to give an account of their structure, or logical form: 'the work of the theory is in relating the known truth-conditions of each sentence to those aspects ("words") of the sentence which recur in other sentences, and can be assigned identical roles in other sentences.'[62] The resulting theory of meaning is explicitly holist: 'the meaning (interpretation) of a sentence is given by assigning the sentence a semantic location in the pattern of sentences that comprise the language.'[63] The power of Davidson's writings lies, aside from their rigour and elegance, in the fact that they provide a realist account of language based on the way in which we use words to talk about the world, while avoiding a narrowly representational account of the relation between words and things. Davidson's theory of meaning has come under formidable attack, notably from Michael Dummett and Hilary Putnam: many of Dummett's criticisms, however, seem to involve a relapse into psychologism and empiricism, and it seems likely that Davidsonian 'formal semantics', subject to certain modifications, will survive the assault.[64] Realism has thus been provided with significant support by the philosophy of language.

(4) Discourse and Practice

A truth-conditional theory of meaning gives a formal and structural account of language: 'what a theory of truth does for a natural language is reveal a structure.'[65] Such an account may be valid as an explanation of how expressions are assigned their sense and reference, and can probably be extended to deal with the force with which utterances are taken (as commands, assertions, etc.). It is, however, only an imperfect guide to the study of linguistic usage, and of its imbrication in social practice. This is not because, as communication-intention theorists claim, the formal semanticists ignore the role of intention and convention in linguistic usage, but rather because linguistic practice typically issues in *discourse*, bodies of utterances or inscriptions larger than a single sentence but smaller than a total language.[66] A formal-semantical analysis of a discourse will be able to give the truth-conditions of the sentences it contains, but will not be able to account for the specific identity the discourse itself may possess. The reason is that formal semanticists, like analytical philosophers generally, are concerned with the *logical form* of expressions, conceived at the very least analogically to the structure of first-order logic. Now logic is concerned with valid inference; it appraises arguments in terms of their structure, independently of the content (but not of the truth-value) of the sentences related in a particular inference. Entirely justifiably, it is not concerned with the question of whether or not there are relations between sentences other than those which transmit truth or falsity.

The attribution to language of the structure of logic may be justified as part of an attempt to model speakers' general capacity to use language; its effect, however, has been that analytical philosophers tend to conceive of the relations between sentences in formal, syntactical terms, failing to register the existence of a middle term between the sentence and the entire language. An exception is Wittgenstein's concept of language-game, which seems to suffer from the fault of identifying language too directly with other social practices, and in any case has been taken to licence either the mere description of ordinary usage, or a conventionalist account of meaning. Even speech-act theory is concerned only with particular *types* of utterances, rather than with definite bodies of utterances, while philosophers of science have until recently tended to concentrate on explicating the logical structure of scientific laws in isolation from the theoretical contexts in which they are constructed. It has been left to philosophers at some remove from the analytical tradition to pose the question of discourse in the English-speaking world: two examples are Collingwood's concept of the 'absolute presuppositions' to which sciences owe their unity, and Lakatos's methodology of scientific research programmes, where the heuristic give theoretical discourses a unity wider than that of the isolated hypothesis.[67] Both of these concepts bear a relation to Althusser's concept of the problematic that constitutes every theoretical discourse, '*the objective reference system of its particular* themes, the system of *questions* that command the *answers* given' (FM 67n).

The failure to theorize the existence of discourses is closely connected to a second absence in analytical philosophy, *history*. Thus, even English-speaking philosophers' discussions of the history of philosophy tend to isolate the doctrine under examination from the theoretical presuppositions that the earlier thinker would have made but his analytical interlocutors do not, on the ground that, in Hide Ishiguro's words, 'the history of philosophy is considered an integral part of philosophy only to the extent that the study of the texts and thoughts of past philosophers contributes to the articulation of philosophical ideas'.[68] The result is frequent misunderstanding: thus, Anthony Kenny shows that the lengthy debates over whether Descartes's *cogito ergo sum* is a syllogism (involving major and minor premises and a conclusion) simply ignore the fact that Descartes, reared in scholastic metaphysics, would have presupposed as self-evident a principle which provides the *cogito* with the major premiss it requires to be a syllogism but appears to lack.[69] The blindness of analytical philosophers to the history of their own discipline is part of a more general refusal to consider the phenomenon of conceptual change, of the systematic transformations in our beliefs which the history of the sciences shows to have occurred. The effect can be the nakedly apologetic cult of common sense characteristic of ordinary language philosophy at its worst, as in Austin's notorious statement:

> Our common stock of words embodies all the distinctions men have found worth drawing, and the connexions they have found worth making, in the lifetimes of many generations; these surely are likely to be more numerous, more sound, since they have stood up to the long test of the survival of the fittest, and more subtle, at least in all ordinary and reasonably practical matters, than any you and I are likely to think up in our armchairs of an afternoon.[70]

Strawson's Kantian version of ordinary language philosophy, a 'descriptive metaphysics . . . aiming to lay bare the most general features of our conceptual structure', is concerned with the 'massive central core of human thinking which has no history'.[71]

The conceptual conservatism of this approach is implicit in the analytical tradition's conception of philosophical method, the dissolution of philosophical problems through the analysis of ordinary language. The discrepancy between the recondite meanings given words by pre-analytical philosophers and their everyday usage reveals, according to Richard Rorty (in his days as an orthodox analytical philosopher), that 'philosophers' premisses are either (a) dubious or plainly false (when the expressions they contain are construed in ordinary ways) or (b) implicit proposals for the reform of language'. Option (b) does not contain a means of escape for the erring metaphysician for 'a specialist may have the right to use jargon when he begins to *answer* questions, but not in the formulation of those primordial questions which originally impelled him to inquire'.[72] But the lesson of the work of philosophers of science such as Bachelard and Lakatos is that the decisive point in the development of a new theoretical discourse is the formulation of new questions, and that, of necessity, this step involves either the invention of a new vocabulary adequate to these questions, or frequently using existing terminology to express the new questions, with the effect of peculiar conceptual torsions and confusions as the novel heuristic struggles out from beneath its old clothing. Every major scientific discovery – those of Copernicus, Galileo, Newton, Marx, Darwin, Freud, and Einstein in particular – involved a challenge to common sense. Our everyday beliefs are in part the product of these breakthroughs; to make them the benchmark by which to judge new theories would be to place a halter on scientific progress. This is not to favour the fashionable, and equally conservative relativism whose response to the fact of conceptual change is to treat us as prisoners of our current 'paradigm', or 'conceptual scheme', unable rationally to criticize it or to compare it with its predecessors; it is only possible to be conscious of discontinuities in our beliefs against the background of underlying continuities.[73] But I think we must view with scepticism G. A. Cohen's recent claim that 'since philosophy of the analytical kind is particularly good at correcting misconstrual, at clarifying the structure of concepts we possess but are disposed to mishandle, it follows that it can be a potent solvent of at least some ideological illusions'.[74] Or, perhaps better, we should insist that analytical techniques can only serve the cause of *Ideologiekritik* as part of a broader methodology which analyses concepts in their historical constellations.

So far I have presented the limitations of analytical philosophy as if discourses could be individualized, their historical patterns traced, without reference to the social formation as a whole. But once we have ceased to consider the theory of sense, and concern ourselves with specific bodies of utterances made in definite circumstances, with language interwoven with other social practices, then the question of the relations of *power* in which discourses are imbricated is posed. 'Power' here refers both to the global system of class domination of which discourses are part, and the relations of power immanent in discursive practices themselves. It is, of course, the recent work of Michel Foucault that has made the latter issue, that of 'power-knowledge', a major theme of philosophical discussion.[75] Finally, there is the question of the *subject*. It is a valid reproach to both Marxism and analytical philosophy that, while their tendency is to deny the subject a constitutive role, they do so while neglecting the processes through which the subject itself is formed, passing this problem over to disciplines such as psychology. But, unless we are prepared to reinstate the concept of a largely unchanging human nature, it would seem appropriate to ask whether subjectivity itself is a product of social practice. This question is to some degree broached in Althusser's work on ideology: it is raised explicitly in Lacan and Foucault's writings, in other respects very different. Both claim that the process of production of discourse shapes and forms individuals into subjects. Without such an approach, Colin McCabe argues, 'the term "discourse" no longer indicates the site(s) of the articulation of language and sociality but simply functions so as to cover for a linguistic formalism or as a sociological formalism'.[76]

These issues – discourse, history, power, the subject – return us to our discussion of ideology in the first section of this chapter, where we concluded by accepting Göran Therborn's redefinition of ideology as the primarily discursive practices through which human beings live their relation to reality. It does not follow that the work of Lacan, Foucault, and other post-structuralists can simply be recuperated within a classical Marxist framework. Lacan's account of the formation of the subject within language makes no reference to history, while Foucault treats relations of power as constitutive of social life, reducing everything from production to the articulations of sentences in discourse to their epiphenomena. On the other hand, the base-superstructure model does not seem terribly helpful when applied to cultural phenomena, beyond the methodological function of reaffirming the explanatory primacy of the relations of production within historical materialism. It gives little or no guidance as to how ideologies are formed, nor to the roles they play within particular social formations.

The Marxist theoretician whose work is most relevant to these questions is Gramsci. His anti-naturalist and anti-realist philosophical views led him to deny that theories have a role other than as the articulation of interests, and thereby to abandon the epistemological conception of ideology which had hitherto dominated Marxism. At the same time, his Hegelian reduction of the social whole to the expressions of a single essence led him to reject the base-superstructure model. He related the formation of ideologies directly to social practice. Every class position within the relations of production, he argued, carries with it a certain conception of the world implicit in the practice of that class. The class struggle involves, among other things, a clash of these conceptions. The dominant class must, in order to secure its monopoly of the means of production and of coercion, fully articulate its conception of the world, which requires the formation or recruitment of a layer of intellectuals, and employ a variety of institutions (churches, political parties, schools, etc.) in order to impose the conception on the masses. The resulting 'dominant ideology' is a complex formation, since the ruling class's conception of the world, in superimposing itself upon that of the dominated classes, will almost certainly absorb and integrate within itself elements of this defeated conception, as well as that of previous ruling classes.

The complexity of the prevailing ideological system will be reflected in the consciousness of the masses, in part because their daily practice gives sustenance to an alternative, subversive conception of the world:

> The active man-in-the-mass has a practical activity, but has no clear theoretical consciousness of his practical activity, which nonetheless involves understanding the world insofar as it transforms it. His theoretical consciousness can indeed be historically in opposition to his activity. One might almost say that he has two theoretical conscious-nesses (or one contradictory consciousness): one which is implicit in his activity and which in reality unites him with all his fellow workers in the practical transformation of the real world; and one, superficially explicit or verbal, which he has inherited from the past and uncritically absorbed.[77]

Socialist consciousness is implicit in workers' daily activity, as they co-operate as the 'collective worker' formed in the labour-process by the development of capitalism, and as they unite to defend themselves against exploitation. The task of the revolutionary party is to make this consciousness explicit. This is possible to the extent that the socialist conception of the world has already been articulated, rendered coherent and systematic by revolutionary intellectuals such as Marx and Engels, themselves responding to the development of the working-class movement and the socialist aspirations it has generated.

There are obviously many questionable elements in this account of ideology. Gramsci's pragmatist epistemology, ironically the means which enabled him to break with earlier Marxist approaches to the question, led him to underestimate the distance between theoretical discourses and everyday experience, and to slide over the question of how a social practice contains implicit within itself a particular conception of the world. Furthermore, he tended to adopt the view that ideology is the cement of social life, a view which we have already found reasons to question. Nevertheless, his approach to the problem of ideology seems unquestionably superior to the available alternatives. It highlights the fact that class domination is not something that automatically arises from the economic base, but has to be *organized*, the constantly contested result of an endless struggle between exploiter and exploited.[78] Furthermore, by breaking down 'ideology', changing it from a self-coherent substance into a series of conceptions of the world imbricated in social practice and the class struggle, Gramsci makes it easier to ask empirical questions about the material determination of ideologies and the role they play in securing, or undermining relations of class domination in specific social formations. It is through the confrontation of Gramsci's thought with theories of discourse that further progress in the Marxist theory of ideology will be made.

Conclusion

On 24 February 1968 Louis Althusser read a communication to the Société Française de Philosophie on 'Lenin and Philosophy'. He began by informing his audience of professional philosophers, who became increasingly angry and restive in the course of the paper, that 'there is no such thing as philosophical communication, no such thing as philosophical discussion'.[1] Philosophy is not a scientific discipline; it has neither an object nor a history, and produces no knowledge. It is, as Kant put it, a *Kampfplatz*, in which two great tendencies, materialism and idealism, fight it out. Philosophy's identity comes from outside itself, from the practices – the sciences and politics – which meet in it. It is 'the class struggle in theory'.[2] It is characteristic of philosophy, however, that it should deny this, its real status. 'What is new in Marxism's contribution to philosophy is a new *practice of philosophy*,' one which openly admits its extra-discursive source in the class struggle.[3]

It is easy to dismiss this argument as a reaction on Althusser's part to his earlier canonization of philosophy as the 'theory of theoretical practice', as a reflection of the impact of the Chinese cultural revolution on the Parisian intelligentsia in the late 1960s, as an anticipation of the events of May-June 1968. It is also easy to point out some of the crudities in Althusser's later definition of philosophy. Thus, it is clear that materialism, which Althusser understands in much the same terms as we have used 'realism' here, is perfectly compatible with conservative political views: this is especially clear in the case of Imre Lakatos, whose methodology of scientific programmes was part of a 'practice of philosophy' aimed at the student New Left and progressive educational theories.[4] Nevertheless, Althusser's intervention has a lasting importance as an attempt radically to question the status of philosophy. We have seen that Marx's and Engels's attempt to 'leap out' of philosphy into science failed. This was clearly, to a large degree, a result of political problems: metaphysical theories were invoked by later Marxists to provide a guarantee of the truth of Marxism and of the inevitability of socialism. Philosophy resumed its traditional role of founding knowledge. But in the work of Adorno and Althusser there is something more, an awareness that we can no longer take accepted notions of thought and reality for granted. This is partly because of developments in the sciences. Marx himself initiated a process, continued by Nietzsche and Freud, which has drastically undermined the notion of reason as *theoria*, the disinterested contemplation of an objective reality:[5] it is now seen to harbour within itself, the class struggle, relations of power, repressed desires. Relativity theory and quantum mechanics have transformed our conceptions of physical reality, biology our conceptions of living beings. Philosophers of science and of language have demolished the view of thought as in any simple sense a representation of reality.

As part of this general challenge to traditional modes of thinking, the notion of philosophical knowledge has come into question. The classical thinkers of the seventeenth century, Galileo, Descartes, Newton, Locke, Leibniz, conceived knowledge as *proven* knowledge: a proposition was true when it was derived from self-evident premisses. But once we challenge the notion of self-evident truths known by the light of reason or experience, knowledge is threatened with an infinite regress, climbing upwards endlessly from conclusion to premiss to further premiss. Hegel sought to halt this 'bad infinity' by transforming science into a circle, generating reality from its own categories. The method of conceptual analysis is another way of stopping the regress: philosophy no longer founds knowledge on self-evident first principles, but instead resolves traditional metaphysical problems by revealing their inconsistency with 'the massive central core of human thinking which has no history', and which is revealed in ordinary usage. We have already exposed the obvious intellectual and political conservatism of such a conception of philosophical method. Contemporary philosophers of science have taken another course. Reversing the pattern of inference, they argue that the sciences are validated through the movement, not from premiss to conclusion, but from conclusion to premiss, stressing that theories are not proved, but *disproved*. The result is a conception of knowledge which stresses the *discontinuities* in our thought. This has been at a price: knowledge is no longer certain, but is fallible, always open to refutation, while the notion of philosophy *founding* the sciences is hopelessly compromised.[6]

Considered in this light, Althusser's propositions have

something to be said for them. Take, for example, his claim that philosophy consists of dogmatically stated theses which are not true or false, but correct or incorrect.[7] Once we abandon the idea of self-evident truths, there is a difficulty about how philosophical propositions may be verified or falsified. It is not solved by Kant's notion of transcendental logic, since, as Hegel pointed out, an enquiry devoted to setting limits to reason presupposes that 'we must know the faculty of knowledge before we can know'.[8] In so far as philosophical propositions are metaphysical statements, not admitting of empirical corroboration and refutation, there seem to be no *a priori* means of establishing their truth or falsity, unless (a) they form part of a scientific research programme, which is not true of such broad epistemological theses as realism, naturalism, etc., or (b) they are logical truths or contradictions, which is very rarely so in the case of any interesting philosophical theory. To this extent, philosophy is indeed a *Kampfplatz*, in which no proposition can ever be definitively proved or disproved, not even Hegelian or Berkeleyan idealism, but, at best, the burden of proof may be shifted onto one's opponent.[9]

Such an account of the status of philosophical propositions does support the notion that philosophical theories derive much of their impetus from terrains external to their discipline, and in particular from the sciences. Popper adopted a position very close to Althusser's when he declared that '*genuine philosophical problems are always rooted in urgent problems outside philosophy, and they die if these roots decay*',[10] proceeding to show how Plato's theory of forms emerged in response to the crisis caused in Greek physics and mathematics by the discovery of irrational numbers. One must be careful to distinguish this from Collingwood's view of philosophy as articulating the 'absolute presuppositions' of existing disciplines, a historicized version of Strawson's 'descriptive metaphysics' easily assimilable into the relativism made fashionable by the discovery of discontinuities in the history of the sciences.[11] Philosophical work can help to precipitate conceptual breakthroughs in the sciences. To quote Althusser, philosophy 'serves as a theoretical laboratory in which the new categories required by the concepts of the new science are brought into focus. For example, was it not in Cartesianism that a new category of causality was worked out for Galilean physics, which had run up against Aristotelian cause as an "epistemological obstacle"?'[12] We can cite other instances of the interaction between philosophy and the sciences. Anti-naturalism, despite, or because of, its idealist premises, resisted the reduction of social relations and discursive formations to the movements of matter and of life championed by nineteenth-century materialism. Frege undertook the philosophical task of polemic and conceptual reformulation necessary if logic was to be cast on a new basis. Contemporary philosophy of language owes much of its impetus to developments in scientific disciplines such as linguistics and mathematical logic.

But what about the class struggle in theory? Even here, there is a large element of truth in Althusser's claims. For there is no doubt that philosophy often serves to dilute conceptual break-throughs, to weaken their impact, to weave them into the seamless coat of Reason, i.e. our 'conceptual scheme', impregnated as it is with the ruling ideology. The response of most professional philosophers to Freud's discovery of the unconscious is one example, the attempt of logical positivists to reduce the new structure of reality revealed by special and general relativity theory to convenient fictions or rules for ordering our experiences is another. Relative to this, Marxist philosophy at its best has been a 'new practice of philosophy', what Adorno called 'the consistent sense of nonidentity' (*ND* 5), thrusting the notion of difference, of a heterogeneous and contradictory reality, into the received harmonies of reason.

But not just the class struggle *in theory*. The bourgeois academy shows the most remarkable ability to recuperate the most *avant garde* of theories. Power can turn the most radical thinker to its own ends. The images of Marx as the icon of a 'really existing socialism' that denies historical materialism's substance as the scientific theory of working-class emancipation, of Nietzsche as the autistic, mustachioed prophet of German fascism, of Freud as the bearded patriarch of 'adaptation' to an oppressive family structure should remind us of this. Lukács, Adorno, and Althusser were all prisoners of their academic specialisms, divorced from the life and activity of the working class. Here we return to the source of Marx's and Engels's original break with philosophy. It was a break with *idealism*, with the proposition that social change is essentially an intellectual process, a battle of ideas. The preoccupation of Western Marxists with ideology has often involved, or led to a version of this theory, the belief that socialist revolution is primarily a matter of ideological struggle, of changing people's ideas. Gramsci is often claimed as the patron of such 'counter-hegemonic strategies'; such an interpretation is, however, quite contrary to the main thrust of his thought.[13] In reality, Gramsci was the Marxist thinker most forcefully to restate Marx's claim in the 'Theses on Feuerbach' that 'the coincidence of the changing of circumstances and of human activity or self-change can be conceived and rationally understood only as *revolutionary practice*' (*CW* 5:4). For since a socialist conception of the world is implicit in the daily practice of the working class, it can only be elicited and rendered dominant over that of the ruling class which is also present in that practice, if revolutionaries actively involve themselves in the struggles of the working class. It was thus that he conceived the revolutionary party, as 'the result of a dialectical process, in which the spontaneous movement of the revolutionary masses and the organizing and directing will of the centre converge'.[14] Outside of such an interaction between theory and practice, party and class, the most brilliant Marxist philosopher is likely to degenerate into the paid jester of the ruling class. The point, after all, is to change the world.

Notes

Introduction

1. See P. Anderson, *Considerations on Western Marxism* (London, 1976).
2. V. I. Lenin, *Collected Works*, xxxviii (Moscow, 1972) 180.
3. Quoted in A. W. Wood, *Karl Marx* (London, Henley, and Boston, 1981) 207.
4. M. Dummett, *Frege: Philosophy of Language* (London, 1973) 683.
5. Quoted in S. Buck-Morss, *The Origins of Negative Dialectics* (Hassocks, 1977) 138–9. To judge by A. J. Ayer's malicious sketch of Adorno in Oxford, the disdain and incomprehension was mutual: see *A Part of My Life* (Oxford, 1977) 153.
6. T. W. Adorno et al., *The Positivist Dispute in German Sociology* (London, 1976). Strictly speaking, Popper cannot be accurately described as an analytical philosopher in the sense given this expression in Chapter 1, since he has always denied that philosophy has anything to do with the analysis of meaning; but he is, by intellectual provenance and family resemblance, closer to this tradition than to any other.
7. P. Anderson, 'Components of the National Culture' in A. Cockburn and R. Blackburn, eds., *Student Power* (Harmondsworth, 1969).
8. P. F. Strawson, *Logico-Linguistic Papers* (London, 1971) 170.
9. See, for example, D.-H. Ruben, *Marxism and Materialism* (Hassocks, 1977), G. A. Cohen, *Karl Marx's Theory of History* (Oxford, 1978), J. Mepham and D.-H. Ruben, eds., *Issues in Marxist Philosophy* (3 vols., Brighton, 1979).
10. See R. Bhaskar, *A Realist Theory of Science* (Hassocks, 1978), B. Hindess, *Philosophy and Methodology in the Social Sciences* (Hassocks, 1977). Alasdair MacIntyre might have been another exception, had he not long since bid Marxism farewell.
11. J. Bouveresse, 'Pourquoi pas des philosophes?', *Critique* XXXIV, no. 369, Feb. 1978, 100.
12. *Critique* XXXVI, no. 399–400, Aug.–Sept. 1980, and no. 409–10, June–July 1981. The article on Davidson in the latter issue is by Pascal Engel.
13. Lukács seems at times to have believed this: see *The Destruction of Reason* (London, 1980).

Chapter 1. Two Traditions

1. A. J. Ayer, *The Central Questions of Philosophy* (Harmondsworth, 1976) 1.
2. W. V. O. Quine, interviewed in B. Magee, ed., *Men of Ideas* (London, 1978) 178. For a similar reply, see J. L. Mackie, *The Cement of the Universe* (Oxford, 1974) 1.
3. E. S. Haldane and G. R. T. Ross, eds., *The Philosophical Works of Descartes* (2 vols., Cambridge, 1970).
4. See A. J. P. Kenny, 'Cartesian Privacy', in G. Pitcher, ed., *Wittgenstein* (London, 1970).
5. See especially Hume, *A Treatise of Human Nature* (Harmondsworth, 1970), Introduction. I draw here on a paper I read to the Oxford Radical Philosophy group on 2 Mar. 1977. See also N. Kemp Smith, *The Philosophy of David Hume* (London, 1949), E. C. Mossner, *David Hume* (Oxford, 1970), and B. Stroud, *David Hume* (London, Boston, and Henley, 1977).
6. Hume, I i 4.
7. Kant, *Logic* (Indianapolis and New York, 1974) 113.
8. Hume, I iv 6.
9. Kant, *The Critique of Judgement* (Oxford, 1973) 19.

10. F. W. J. Schelling, *Philosophical Inquiries into the Nature of Human Freedom and Matters Connected Therewith* (Chicago, 1936) 87.
11. G. W. F. Hegel, *The Phenomenology of Mind* (London, 1966) 79.
12. Kant, *Logic* 14–15.
13. Hegel, *Phenomenology* 115.
14. Ibid. 123.
15. M. Dummett, *Truth and Other Enigmas* (London, 1978) 441. The interpretation of Frege that follows draws heavily, and eclectically, on M. Dummett, *Frege: Philosophy of Language* (London, 1973), D. Bell, *Frege's Theory of Judgement* (Oxford, 1979), and H. Sluga, *Gottlob Frege* (London, 1980). Commentators on Frege are far from agreed: see Sluga, and Dummett's *The Interpretation of Frege's Philosophy* (London, 1981).
17. Dummett, *Frege* 174.
18. Frege, *Posthumous Writings* (Oxford, 1979) 15, 16.
19. See Dummett, *Frege* ch. I, and Sluga, ch. III.
20. D. Davidson, 'Belief and the Basis of Meaning', *Synthese* 27 (1974) 319.
21. B. Russell, 'On Denoting', in Russell, *Logic and Knowledge*, ed. R. C. Marsh (London, 1956).
22. P. F. Strawson, *Logico-Linguistic Papers* (London, 1971) 27.
23. R. Rorty, editor's introduction, *The Linguistic Turn* (Chicago and London, 1967) 12.
24. P. Geach and M. Black, eds. *Translations from the Philosophical Writings of Gottlob Frege* (Oxford, 1970) 57.
25. Dummett, *Frege* 93.
26. Ibid. 88.
27. For a recent survey of such theories, see B. Harrison, *An Introduction to the Philosophy of Language* (London, 1979).
28. G. Frege, *The Foundations of Arithmetic* (Oxford, 1980) x. See Dummett, *Frege* 3 ff., and J. Wallace, 'Only in the context of a sentence do words have any meaning', in P. A. French, T. E. Uehling, and H. E. Wettstein, eds., *Contemporary Perspectives in the Philosophy of Language* (Minneapolis, 1979).
29. Bell, 3.
30. Sluga, 61–2.
31. Kant, *Logic* 106. Emphasis added.
32. L. Wittgenstein, *Philosophical Grammar* (Oxford, 1974) I i 6, 3.
33. See I. Hacking, *Why does Language Matter to Philosophy?* (Cambridge, 1975) 115–56, on the 'heyday of sentences'. I have discussed post-structuralist theories of language in *Is There a Future for Marxism?* (London, 1982), chs. 2, 4, and 7.
34. Rorty, 11.
35. W. V. O. Quine, 'Replies', in D. Davidson and J. Hintikka, eds., *Words and Objections* (Dordrecht, 1969) 333. Emphasis added.
36. D. Davidson, *Essays on Actions and Events* (Oxford, 1980), essays 6 and 7. See the discussion of logical form, ibid. 137 ff.
37. G. Ryle, *The Concept of Mind* (London, 1949).
38. Quine, *Ontological Relativity and Other Essays* (New York and London, 1969) 27, 26.

Chapter 2. The End of Philosophy?

1. The basic work on Marx's development is A. Cornu, *Karl Marx et Friedrich Engels* (4 vols., Paris, 1958–70). Three other outstanding studies are S. Hook, *From Hegel to Marx* (London, 1936), M. Löwy, *La Théorie de la révolution chez le jeune Marx* (Paris, 1970), and, for the broad philosophical background, K. Löwith, *From Hegel to Nietzsche* (London, 1965). Also of interest are D. McLellan, *Karl Marx and the Young Hegelians* (London, 1969) and *Marx before Marxism* (London, 1970), H. Draper, *Karl Marx's Theory of Revolution*, vol. 1 (London, 1977) Part 1, and G. Labica, *Marxism and the Status of Philosophy* (London, 1980).

2. See, on Engels's development, in addition to Cornu, Draper, and Labica, G. Stedman-Jones, 'Engels and the Genesis of Marxism', *New Left Review*, no. 106, Nov.–Dec. 1977, which stresses Engels's precocity relative to Marx and his influence on the latter.
3. G. W. F. Hegel, *Lectures on the History of Philosophy* (3 vols., London, 1963) iii. 546, 547.
4. Löwith, 48.
5. Hegel to Niethammer, 28 Oct. 1808, extract in W. Kaufman, *Hegel* (London, 1965) 323.
6. G. W. F. Hegel, *The Philosophy of Right* (New York, 1971) 10. See G. Lukács, *The Young Hegel* (London, 1975). Herbert Marcuse, however, believed that Hegel's 'reconciliation with reality' dated from the *Phenomenology*: see *Reason and Revolution* (London, 1968) 92.
7. Löwith, 117–18. See also Marcuse, 323 ff.
8. See *CW* 4:139, G. Lukács, *Political Writings 1919–1929* (London, 1972) 193, and Cornu, i. 161.
9. The following draws heavily on M. Wartofsky, *Feuerbach* (Cambridge, 1977).
10. C.-A. Helvétius, *De l'Esprit* (Paris, 1968) 40.
11. See *CW* 1:85, 491, and the excellent discussion of the dissertation in Cornu, i. 183 ff., followed by J.-M. Gabaude in *Le Jeune Marx et le matérialisme antique* (Toulouse, 1970).
12. K. Marx, *A Contribution to the Critique of Political Economy* (London, 1971) 19.
13. Draper, 57.
14. See Althusser's excellent selection and translation, L. Feuerbach, *Manifestes philosophiques* (Paris, 1960), and Cornu, ii. 123–35.
15. Cornu, ii. 288–9. The following paragraphs are heavily indebted to Löwy.
16. See W. Benjamin, *Charles Baudelaire* (London, 1973). For Marx in Paris, see Löwy, 79–120, Cornu, iii, and J. Grandjonc, *Marx et les communistes allemands à Paris 1844* (Paris, 1974).
17. Marx, *Contribution* 20.
18. See L. Althusser, 'Note du traducteur', in Feuerbach, *Manifestes* 5–6.
19. See *CW* 3:276, and, in addition, Hook, 272–307, Allen W. Wood, *Karl Marx* (London, Henley, and Boston, 1981) 32, and E. V. Ilienkov, *Dialectical Logic* (Moscow, 1977) 27–74.
20. J. Habermas, *Knowledge and Human Interests* (London, 1972) 31. See also A. Schmidt, *The Concept of Nature in Marx* (London, 1971) and Althusser's anti-Hegelian concept of practice in *FM* and *RC*.
21. See S. S. Prawer, *Karl Marx and World Literature* (Oxford, 1976), and also L. Kolakowski, *Main Currents of Marxism* (3 vols., Oxford, 1978) i.
22. See I. Mészáros, *Marx's Theory of Alienation* (London, 1970) and B. Ollman, *Alienation* (Cambridge, 1971).
23. See K. R. Popper, *The Logic of Scientific Discovery* (London, 1968), J. W. N. Watkins, 'Confirmable and Influential Metaphysics', *Mind* LXVII (n.s.) July 1958, and I. Lakatos, *Philosophical Papers* (2 vols., Cambridge, 1978) i ch. 1.
24. See Draper, 160 ff., and, on Hess and Engels, Cornu, ii. 304–40.
25. M. Stirner, *The Ego and his Own* (New York, 1973) 40.
26. Ibid., 37.
27. See *CW* 4:126–34, and Löwy, 113–20.
28. See *FM* and, from a very different theoretical standpoint, Löwy, 24, n. 21.
29. For an example of such confusion, see D. Sayer, *Marx's Method* (Hassocks, 1979).
30. On Newton, see Lakatos, i ch. 5.
31. See G. Therborn, *Science, Class, Society* (London, 1976) 355–75, and Labica, 282–4.
32. See *RC*, B. Hindess and P. Hirst, *Precapitalist Modes of Production* (London, 1975), G. A. Cohen, *Karl Marx's Theory of History* (Oxford, 1978), and A. Callinicos, *Is There a Future for Marxism?* (London, 1982).
33. On the Scottish historical school, see R. Meek, 'The Scottish Contribution to Marxist Sociology' in *Economics and Ideology and Other Essays* (London, 1967).
34. See L. Althusser, 'Marx's Relation to Hegel', in *Politics and History* (London, 1972) and *Essays in Self Criticism* (London, 1976).
35. Althusser, *Lenin and Philosophy and Other Essays* (London, 1971) 81.
36. See, for example, Mészáros, Ollman, and D. McLellan, *Karl Marx* (London, 1973). Althusser, Cornu, and Hook are among the main opponents of this interpretation.

37. Wood, 7.
38. Löwith, 92.
39. See L. Colletti, *Marxism and Hegel* (London, 1973), and 'Marxism and the Dialectic', *New Left Review*, no. 93, Sept.–Oct. 1975. See also G. Della Volpe, *Logic as a Positive Science* (London, 1980), and Callinicos, *Is There a Future For Marxism?* ch. 5.
40. See K. R. Popper, *Conjectures and Refutations* (London, 1969) ch. 15.
41. See Hegel's lengthy critique of the calculus, *GL* i. 256–332.
42. See Callinicos, loc. cit., and A. Giddens, *Central Problems in Social Theory* (London, 1979) 131 ff., which contains an excellent critical discussion of the account of contradiction in J. Elster, *Logic and Society* (London, 1978).
43. The following argument has been developed more fully in A. Callinicos, 'The Logic of Capital' (D. Phil. thesis, University of Oxford, 1978).
44. Hegel, *Lectures* ii. 368–9. See also Lakatos ii Part 1.

Chapter 3. The Return of the Repressed

1. Marx, *A Contribution to the Critique of Political Economy* (London, 1971) 22.
2. See G. Stedman-Jones, 'Engels and the End of Classical German Philosophy', *New Left Review*, no. 79, May-June 1973.
3. See G. Lukács, 'The New Edition of Lassalle's Letters' and 'Moses Hess and the Problem of Idealist Dialectics', *Political Writings 1919-1929* (London, 1972).
4. F. Engels, *Dialectics of Nature* (Moscow, 1954) 267.
5. See L. Colletti, *Marxism and Hegel* (London, 1973) and D. Lecourt, *A Proletarian Science?* (London, 1977).
6. K. Kautsky, *The Class Struggle* (New York, 1971) 117.
7. G. V. Plekhanov, *Selected Philosophical Works* (4 vols., Moscow, 1976) i. 483.
8. M. Salvadori, *Karl Kautsky and the Socialist Revolution 1880-1938* (London, 1979) 23. It should be noted that this evolutionist, Darwinist Marxism had little to do with either the theory of evolution or Darwin. Marx noted of the *Origin of Species* that 'not only is the death-blow dealt here for the first time to "teleology" in the natural sciences but its rational meaning is empirically explained' (*SC* 115). See also V. Gerratana, 'Marx and Darwin', *New Left Review*, no. 82, Nov.–Dec. 1973.
9. See C. Schorske, *German Social Democracy, 1905-1917* (Cambridge, Mass., 1955).
10. See A. Gramsci, *Selections from the Prison Notebooks* (London, 1971) 336, and W. Benjamin, *One-Way Street and Other Writings* (London, 1979) 368-70.
11. See Salvadori, 30 ff., 133–46, 152–65.
12. E. Bernstein, *Evolutionary Socialism* (New York, 1967) 197. On the 'Bernsteiniad', see L. Colletti, 'Bernstein and the Marxism of the Second International', in *Rousseau and Lenin* (London, 1972), and P. Gay, *The Dilemma of Democratic Socialism* (New York, 1962).
13. Quoted in Salvadori, 103.
14. Quoted in J. P. Nettl, *Rosa Luxemburg* (2 vols., London, 1966) i. 156.
15. See Y. Bourdet, 'Introduction' to R. Hilferding, *Le Capital financier* (Paris, 1970), T. Bottomore and P. Goode, eds., *Austro-Marxism* (Oxford, 1978), R. Loew, 'The SPÖ: from Hapsburgs to Hitler', *New Left Review*, no. 118, Nov.–Dec. 1979.
16. R. Hilferding, *Finance Capital* (London, Henley, and Boston, 1981) 23–4.
17. Bottomore and Goode, 52.
18. See P. M. S. Hacker, *Insight and Illusion* (Oxford, 1972).
19. Bottomore and Goode, 65.
20. Ibid. 70.
21. Ibid. 68.
22. For one instance of this tendency, Bauer's theory of nationality, see M. Löwy, 'Marxists and the National Question', *New Left Review*, no. 96, Mar.–Apr. 1976.
23. See Nettl, i. 433.
24. On Lenin, see G. Lukács, *Lenin* (London, 1970), T. Cliff, *Lenin* (4 vols., London, 1975-9), M. Liebman, *Leninism under Lenin* (London, 1975), and N. Harding, *Lenin's Political Thought* (2 vols., London, 1977, 1981).

25. See C. Harman, *Party and Class* (London, 1981), H. Weber, *Marxisme et Conscience de Classe* (Paris, 1976), and J. Molineux, *Marxism and the Party* (London, 1978).
26. V. I. Lenin, *Collected Works* (Moscow, 1972) ix. 44.
27. Ibid. v. 368 n.
28. Ibid. xiii. 103–4.
29. A. Gramsci, *Selections from the Political Writings 1910–1920* (London, 1977) 34–7.
30. See F. Gregory, *Scientific Materialism in Nineteenth-Century Germany* (Dordrecht and Boston, 1977).
31. K. Korsch, *Marxism and Philosophy* (London, 1970) 77.
32. See, for example, Gramsci, *Prison Notebooks* 367–8. Compare B. Croce, *Logic as the Science of the Pure Concept* (London, 1917) 332: 'the natural sciences are not directed to action, but are, themselves, actions.'
33. See L. Althusser, *Lenin and Philosophy and Other Essays* (London, 1971), and D. Lecourt, *Une crise et son enjeu* (Paris, 1973).
34. Lenin, xxxviii. 182.
35. Ibid. xxxviii. 360.
36. Ibid. xxi. 236.
37. Lukács, *Lenin* ch. 6. See also Cliff, i ch. 14, and L. Trotsky, *The Third International after Lenin* (New York, 1970) 75 ff.
38. See G. Stedman-Jones, 'The Marxism of the Early Lukács', *New Left Review*, no. 70, Nov.–Dec. 1971, I. Mészáros, *Lukács' Concept of Dialectic* (London, 1972), M. Löwy, *Georg Lukács – From Romanticism to Bolshevism* (London, 1979), and A. Arato and P. Breines, *The Young Lukács and the Origins of Western Marxism* (London, 1979).
39. G. Lukács, 1962 Preface, *The Theory of the Novel* (London, 1978) 19.
40. Löwy, *Lukács* 165.
41. Ibid. 128–64. Löwy argues, unconvincingly, that *History and Class Consciousness* 'opens a new theoretical universe, one that abolishes/transcends the utopian tendencies of 1919–20' (p. 173).
42. See M. Weber, *Economy and Society* (Berkeley, Los Angeles, and London, 1978).
43. Ibid. 1401.
44. Bottomore and Goode, 65.
45. See Arato and Breines, 203 ff., 163–89.
46. See J. Révai, 'Review of *History and Class Consciousness*', first published in *Grunbergs Arkhiv* XI (1925), English translation in *Theoretical Practice*, no. 1, January 1971.
47. See V. Gerratana, 'Stalin, Lenin and "Leninism"', *New Left Review*, no. 103, May–June 1977.
48. L. Trotsky, *The First Five Years of the Communist International* (2 vols., New York, 1972) i. 211.
49. *Documents of the Fourth International: the Formative Years (1933–1940)* (New York, 1973) 182.
50. W. Benjamin, *Illuminations* (London, 1970) 260.
51. See P. Anderson, *Considerations on Western Marxism* (London, 1976).
52. Benjamin, *Illuminations* 263, 259–60. Klee's painting was one of Benjamin's most prized possessions: see G. Scholem, 'Walter Benjamin and his Angel' in *On Jews and Judaism in Crisis* (New York, 1976).
53. T. W. Adorno, 'The Actuality of Philosophy', *Telos*, no. 31, Spring 1977, 120. See also M. Horkheimer, *Critical Theory* (New York, 1972) 210–11.
54. See, for example, M. Horkheimer, 'On the Problem of Truth', in A. Arato and E. Gebhardt, eds., *The Frankfurt School Reader* (Oxford, 1978). On the Frankfurt School generally, see M. Jay, *The Dialectical Imagination* (London, 1973), and D. Held, *Introduction to Critical Theory* (London, 1980).
55. Horkheimer, *Critical Theory* 213–14.
56. Benjamin, *Illuminations* 262.
57. M. Horkheimer, *Eclipse of Reason* (New York, 1947) 41.
58. M. Horkheimer and T. W. Adorno, *Dialectic of Enlightenment* (London, 1973) 88.
59. Ibid. 90.

60. See, especially, G. Deleuze, *Différence et répétition* (Paris, 1969).
61. See G. Della Volpe, *Logic as a Positive Science* (London, 1980) and Colletti, *Marxism and Hegel.* Robert Paris's introduction to G. Della Volpe, *Rousseau et Marx* (Paris, 1974) is very helpful. The title of J. Fraser, *Introduction to the Thought of Galvano Della Volpe* (London, 1977) is misleading, since it is, if anything, more difficult than the writings it is supposed to make accessible.
62. M. Jay, 'The Concept of Totality in Lukács and Adorno', *Telos*, no. 32, Summer 1977, 136.
63. See Löwy, *Lukács* 193–204, Arato and Breines, 190 ff., and F. Feher, 'Lukács in Weimar', *Telos*, no. 39, Spring 1979.
64. E. Bloch *et al.*, *Aesthetics and Politics* (London, 1977) 176.
65. Lukács, *Theory* 22.
66. T. W. Adorno, *Minima Moralia* (London, 1974) 50.
67. Ibid. 74.
68. On the relationship between Adorno and Benjamin, see M. Rosen, 'The Rationality of Hegel's Dialectic and its Criticisms' (D. Phil. thesis, University of Oxford, 1980) ch. 7, and S. Buck-Morss, *The Origins of Negative Dialectics* (Hassocks, 1977). See also, T. Eagleton, *Walter Benjamin, Or Towards a Revolutionary Criticism* (London, 1981).
69. M. Rosen, 'Walter Benjamin and the Tradition', paper presented to the course 'Marxismus und Phänomenologie', IUC Dubrovnik, March 1978, 8.
70. Quoted in T. W. Adorno, *Prisms* (London, 1967) 231.
71. Benjamin, *One-Way Street* 117–18.
72. Ibid. 160.
73. W. Benjamin, 'Epistemo-Critical Prologue', *The Origins of German Tragic Drama* (London, 1977) 27–56. See the discussion of the Marxist version of this theory in S. Buck-Morss, 'Walter Benjamin – Revolutionary Writer' (I), *New Left Review*, no. 128, July–Aug. 1981.
74. Adorno, *Prisms* 236. The main texts of the Adorno-Benjamin debate are reproduced with an introduction by Perry Anderson in Bloch *et al.*, 100–41. See also W. Benjamin, *Charles Baudelaire* (London, 1973).
75. T. W, Adorno, 'Sociology and Empirical Research', in Adorno *et al.*, *The Positivist Dispute in German Sociology* (London, 1976) 80.
76. Quoted in Benjamin, *Origins* 27. See also H. Marcuse, *Eros and Civilization* (London, 1972) chs. 5, 8, and 9.
77. Horkheimer, *Eclipse* 179.
78. See W. Benjamin, 'Surrealism', in *One-Way Street*, especially the passage advocating 'metaphysical materialism, of the brand of Vogt and Bukharin', 236.
79. See Adorno *et al.*, *passim*, and also Horkheimer, 'Traditional and Critical Theory', Horkheimer, *Critical Theory*.
80. J. Habermas, *Knowledge and Human Interest* (London, 1972) 32–3.
81. I have discussed Althusser at length in *Althusser's Marxism* (London, 1976) and *Is There a Future for Marxism?* (London, 1982). See also the special issue of *Dialectiques* on Althusser, no. 15–16, Autumn 1976.
82. For a critical discussion of Althusser's concept of 'differential temporality', see P. Anderson, *Arguments within English Marxism* (London, 1980) 73–7.
83. See D. Caute, *Communism and the French Intellectuals 1914-60* (London, 1964), and Lecourt, *A Proletarian Science?*
84. For an extension of this concept of practice to aesthetic theory, see P. Macherey, *A Theory of Literary Production* (London, Henley, and Boston, 1978) and T. Eagleton, *Literature and Ideology* (London, 1976).
85. See D. Lecourt, *Marxism and Epistemology* (London, 1976), and *Bachelard – ou, le jour et la nuit* (Paris, 1974).
86. Althusser, *Politics and History* (London, 1972) 77–8.
87. See Althusser, 'Ideology and the Ideological State Apparatuses', in *Lenin and Philosophy*.
88. See J. Rancière, 'On the Theory of Ideology', *Radical Philosophy*, no. 7, Spring 1974, and P. Hirst, 'Althusser and the Theory of Ideology', in *On Law and Ideology* (London, 1979).
89. See E. Balibar, 'Sur le dialectique historique', *Pensée*, no. 170, Aug. 1973, B. Hindess and P. Hirst, *Precapitalist Modes of Production* (London, 1975) 272–8, and Callinicos, *Future* 129–34.

90. See Callinicos, *Althusser's Marxism* ch. 3.
91. Althusser, *Essays in Self-Criticism* (London, 1976) 169.

Chapter 4. Materialism and Naturalism

1. See W. V. O. Quine, 'On What There Is' in *From a Logical Point of View* (New York, 1963), and *Ontological Relativity and Other Essays* (New York and London, 1969).
2. For a representative sample of this argument, see L. Goldmann, *The Human Sciences and Philosophy* (London, 1969).
3. See, for an excellent discussion of Marx's views on the relation between man and nature, V. Gerratana, 'Marx and Darwin', *New Left Review*, no. 82, Nov.–Dec. 1973.
4. A. Collier, 'Materialism and Explanation in the Human Sciences', in J. Mepham and D.-H. Ruben, eds., *Issues in Marxist Philosophy* (3 vols., Brighton, 1979) ii.
5. A. Callinicos, *Is There a Future for Marxism?* (London, 1982) chs. 5–7.
6. Allen Wood is, therefore, quite wrong to describe Marx's treatment of the relation between man and nature in the *Manuscripts* as 'parallel' to Hegel's: see A. W. Wood, *Karl Marx* (London, Henley, and Boston, 1981) 170.
7. See M. Horkheimer and T. W. Adorno, *Dialectic of Enlightenment* (London, 1973) and M. Horkheimer, *Eclipse of Reason* (New York, 1947).
8. W. Benjamin, *One-Way Street and Other Writings* (London, 1979) 103–4.
9. S. Timpanaro, *On Materialism* (London, 1976) 65. Collier takes a similar line.
10. Ibid. 80.
11. See two excellent discussions of Timpanaro: R. Williams, 'Problems of Materialism' in *Problems in Materialism and Culture* (London, 1980), and K. Soper, 'Marxism, Materialism and Biology', in Mepham and Ruben, ii.
12. S. Hook, 'A Personal Impression of Contemporary German Philosophy', *Journal of Philosophy*, XXVII:6, Mar. 1930, 147.
13. See F. Ringer, *The Decline of the German Mandarins* (Cambridge, Mass., 1969).
14. See L. Colletti, *Marxism and Hegel* (London, 1973). See the devastating critique of Frankfurt Marxism's incomprehension of logic and natural science in A. MacIntyre, *Marcuse* (London, 1970) ch. 7.
15. Hume, *Dissertation on the Passions*, quoted in E. C. Mossner, *The Life of David Hume* (Oxford, 1970) 71, n. 1.
16. Adam Smith, *An Inquiry into the Nature and Causes of the Wealth of Nations* (Harmondsworth, 1973) 117.
17. W. V. O. Quine, 'Facts of the Matter', in R. W. Shahan and C. Swoyer, eds., *Essays in the Philosophy of W. V. Quine* (Hassocks, 1979) 169.
18. See D. Davidson, *Essays on Actions and Events* (Oxford, 1980) Essays 11–13.
19. See H.-G. Gadamer, *Truth and Method* (London, 1975).
20. M. Weber, *Economy and Society* (Berkeley, Los Angeles, and London, 1978) 4. See W. G. Runciman, *A Critique of Max Weber's Philosophy of Social Science* (Cambridge, 1972.
21. See C. Taylor, 'Interpretation and the Sciences of Man', *Review of Metaphysics*, 25 (1971) 24–9.
22. Taylor, 'Understanding in Human Science', ibid. 34 (1980) 33–4.
23. Taylor, 'Understanding and Explanation in the *Geisteswissenschaften*', in S. H. Holtzmann and C. M. Leich, eds., *Wittgenstein: to Follow a Rule* (London, Boston, and Henley, 1981) 193.
24. P. Pettit, 'Evaluative "Realism" and Interpretation', ibid. 212. See also J. McDowell, 'Non-Cognitivism and Rule-Following', ibid., and M. Platts, *Ways of Meaning* (London, Henley, and Boston, 1979) ch. X.
25. Taylor, 'Understanding and Explanation' 205.
26. Ibid. 200, 197–8. See, in addition to the texts cited in note 24 above, A. MacIntyre, *After Virtue* (London, 1981) and B. Williams, *Moral Luck* (Cambridge, 1981).
27. G. Macdonald and P. Pettit, *Semantics and Social Science* (London, Henley, and Boston, 1981).

28. Ibid. 65.
29. Ibid. 94–100.
30. Functionalist versions of Marxism are to found in G. A. Cohen, *Karl Marx's Theory of History* (Oxford, 1978), and in Wood. There are excellent critiques of functionalism in J. Elster, *Logic and Society* (London, 1978), and A. Giddens, *Central Problems of Social Theory* (London, 1979).
31. Giddens, *Central Problems*, and *New Rules of Sociological Method* (London, 1976). See also R. Bhaskar, *The Possibility of Naturalism* (Brighton, 1979).
32. Giddens, *Central Problems* 189. See also the discussion of 'interests' in S. Lukes, *Power* (London, 1974). Göran Therborn wishes to eliminate the notion of 'motivation by interest' from Marxism as a 'normative concept', *The Ideology of Power and the Power of Ideology* (London, 1980) 4–5, 10. But, first, we have seen that social science is irreducibly evaluative, and, secondly, the only alternative to the notion of interests as a link between objective relations of production and conscious action would seem to be some version of functionalism, into which Therborn falls when he treats 'the formation of humans by every ideology' as 'a process simultaneously of subjection and of qualification', ibid. 17.
33. K. Marx, 'Marginal Notes on Adolph Wagner's *Lehrbuch der politischen Ökonomie*', *Theoretical Practice*, no. 5, Spring 1972, 52.
34. Cohen, 151. See Callinicos, *Future* 144–5, and A. Levine and E. O. Wright, 'Rationality and Class Struggle', *New Left Review*, no. 123, Sept.–Oct. 1980. I have benefited greatly from hearing Mike Rosen read a paper on Cohen's reconstruction of Marx.
35. Cohen, 134.
36. Ibid. 152, 153.
37. See G. Bois, *Crise du féodalisme* (Paris, 1976).
38. Cohen, 156.
39. Ibid. 162.
40. Ibid. 134.

Chapter 5. Materialism and Realism

1. Lenin, *Materialism and Empirio-Criticism* (Moscow, 1947) 116.
2. See H. Putnam, *Meaning and the Moral Sciences* (London, Henley, and Boston, 1978) 34–5. It is realism in this sense that is at issue in contemporary moral philosophy and philosophy of language.
3. D.-H. Ruben, *Marxism and Materialism* (Hassocks, 1977) 19.
4. See Lenin, 122, 250, and Engels, *Anti-Dühring* (Moscow, 1969) 103 ff.
5. S. Hook, *From Hegel to Marx* (London, 1936) 284, and L. Kolakowski, 'Karl Marx and the Classical Definition of Truth' in *Marxism and Beyond* (London, 1971).
6. S. Hook, *Towards an Understanding of Karl Marx* (London, 1933) 95.
7. Lenin, *Selected Works* (Moscow, 1968) 20. See also Ruben, 76 ff., 193–7, and Allen W. Wood, *Karl Marx* (London, Henley, and Boston) 182–6.
8. See P. Jacob, *L'Empirisme logique* (Paris, 1980) 256–79.
9. See J. Mepham and D.-H. Ruben, eds., *Issues in Marxist Philosophy* (3 vols., Brighton, 1979) i.
10. See R. Harré and E. Madden, *Causal Powers* (Oxford, 1975), and R. Bhaskar, *A Realist Theory of Science* (Hassocks, 1978).
11. See S. Kripke, 'Naming and Necessity', and K. Donnellan, 'Proper Names and Identifying Descriptions', in D. Davidson and G. Harman, eds., *The Semantics of Natural Languages* (Dordrecht and Boston, 1972), H. Putnam, *Mind, Language and Reality* (Cambridge, 1975), and S. P. Schwartz, ed., *Naming, Necessity and Natural Kinds* (Ithaca and London, 1979).
12. See Jacob, 226 ff.
13. H. Putnam, 'Meaning and Reference' in Schwartz, 132.
14. R. Rorty, *Philosophy and the Mirror of Nature* (Oxford, 1980) 294.
15. D. Papineau, *Theory and Meaning* (Oxford, 1979) 125.
16. A. Callinicos, *Is There a Future for Marxism?* (London, 1982) ch. 7.

17. Rorty, 7.
18. W. V. O. Quine, *From a Logical Point of View* (New York, 1963) 20.
19. Quine, 'Carnap and Logical Truth' in P. A. Schilpp, ed., *The Philosophy of Rudolph Carnap* (La Salle and London, 1963) 406.
20. D. Davidson, 'Belief and the Basis of Meaning', *Synthese* 27 (1974) 322.
21. P. Duhem, *The Aim and Structure of Physical Theory* (Princeton, 1954) 187.
22. Ibid. 199–200.
23. Quine, 42. Davidson suggests that Quine remains a captive of a 'third dogma' of empiricism, closely bound up with the other two, namely, 'the dualism of conceptual scheme and empirical content', of 'organizing system and something waiting to be organized': 'On the Very Idea of a Conceptual Scheme', *Proceedings and Addresses of the American Philosophical Association*. XLVII (1973–4) 11.
24. M. Dummett, *Frege: Philosophy of Language* (London, 1973) 623, 592.
25. F. Jameson, *The Prison-House of Language* (Princeton, 1974) 32–3. See also Callinicos, *Future* ch. 2.
26. Rorty, 59.
27. Ibid. 142 ff.
28. K. R. Popper, *The Logic of Scientific Discovery* (London, 1968) 93.
29. See A. Callinicos, *Althusser's Marxism* (London, 1976) ch. 3, E. P. Thompson, 'The Poverty of Theory', in *The Poverty of Theory and Other Essays* (London, 1978), and P. Anderson, *Arguments within English Marxism* (London, 1980) ch. 1.
30. I. Lakatos, *Philosophical Papers* (2 vols., Cambridge, 1975) i. 47.
31. Ibid. 50.
32. Ibid. 16.
33. I. Hacking, 'Imre Lakatos's Philosophy of Science', *British Journal for the Philosophy of Science* 30 (1979) 383.
34. Rorty, 159, 332–3.
35. See Papineau, 125 ff.
36. Lakatos specifically endorsed Engels's and Lenin's philosophical views, ii. 125. I have discussed his claim that Marxism is a degenerating research programme (ibid. i ch. 1) in Callinicos, *Future* ch. 8.

Chapter 6. Language and Ideology

1. Marx, *A Contribution to the Critique of Political Economy* (London, 1971) 21.
2. M. Jay, *The Dialectical Imagination* (London, 1973) 166.
3. J. Habermas, *Communication and the Evolution of Society* (London, 1979) 120.
4. K. Korsch, *Marxism and Philosophy* (London, 1970) 77.
5. A. Gramsci, *Selections from the Prison Notebooks* (London, 1971) 57.
6. For a sample of such thinking see S. Carrillo, 'Eurocommunism' and the State (London, 1977).
7. A. Callinicos, *Althusser's Marxism* (London, 1976) 96 ff. The following discussion owes much to my reading of an unpublished paper on fetishism and ideology by Michael Rosen, and of G. Therborn, *The Ideology of Power and the Power of Ideology* (London, 1980). See also J. Larrain, *The Concept of Ideology* (London, 1979), for an excellent general survey of the subject.
8. See I. I. Rubin, *Essays on Marx's Theory of Value* (Detroit, 1972) and J. Rancière, 'Le Concept de critique et la critique de l'économie politique dès les *Manuscrits de 1844* au *Capital*', in L. Althusser et al., *Lire le Capital* (4 vols., Paris, 1973).
9. Rancière, 82.
10. See P. Hirst, *On Law and Ideology* (London, 1979) ch. 4, and B. Brewster, 'Fetishism in *Capital* and *Reading Capital*', *Economy and Society*, vol. 5, no. 3, Aug. 1976.
11. See A. Callinicos, *Is There a Future for Marxism?* (London, 1982) 119–29.
12. See C. A. Cohen, *Karl Marx's Theory of History* (Oxford, 1978) ch. 5.
13. Marx, 'The Value-Form', *Capital and Class*, no. 4, Spring 1978, 140.

14. Rancière, 50. See CW 4:57–61.
15. E. Bloch et al., Aesthetics and Politics (London, 1977) 111.
16. Much the same position is adopted by Lucio Colletti, for example, in his Introduction to Marx, Early Writings (Harmondsworth, 1975).
17. Bloch et al., 129.
18. S. Buck-Morss, The Origins of Negative Dialectics (Hassocks, 1977) 96.
19. But see T. Eagleton, Walter Benjamin, Or Towards a Revolutionary Criticism (London, 1981) 176–7 on Benjamin's incipient 'culturalism'.
20. See N. Abercrombie, S. Hill, and B. S. Turner, The Dominant Ideology Thesis (London, 1980).
21. Therborn, 2. See n. 32 of ch. 4 above, for a reservation concerning this account of ideology.
22. There is some overlap between ideology thus conceived and Raymond Williams's concept of cultural practices; see Marxism and Literature (Oxford, 1977) and Problems in Materialism and Culture (London, 1980).
23. V. N. Volosinov, Marxism and the Philosophy of Language (New York and London, 1973).
24. See G. Deleuze, Logique du sens (Paris, 1969).
25. L. Wittgenstein, Philosophical Investigations (Oxford, 1968) I 111, 92.
26. See D. Bell, Frege's Theory of Judgement (Oxford, 1979) 79, on Frege's 'essentially mundane' approach to language.
27. See K. R. Popper, Objective Knowledge (Oxford, 1972).
28. I. Hacking, 'Imre Lakatos's Philosophy of Science', British Journal for the Philosophy of Science, 30 (1979) 394.
29. My formulation of the issue in these terms is greatly indebted to V. Descombes, Le Même et l'autre (Paris, 1979).
30. J. Lacan, 'The Agency of the Letter in the Unconscious since Freud', in Écrits: a Selection (London, 1977).
31. D. Davidson, 'What Metaphors Mean', in M. Platts, ed., Reference, Truth and Reality (London, 1980) 240.
32. Lacan, loc. cit.
33. F. Jameson, The Prison-House of Language (Princeton, 1974) 122.
34. See, for example, J. Derrida, Of Grammatology (Baltimore, 1976) and Writing and Difference (London and Henley, 1978).
35. See, in particular, G. Deleuze, Différence et répétition (Paris, 1969).
36. Elie Zahar first pointed this out to me.
37. See Callinicos, Future, passim, and P. Dews, 'The Nouvelle Philosophie and Foucault', Economy and Society, vol. 8, no. 2, May 1979.
38. Wittgenstein, Investigations I 43.
39. M. Dummett, Truth and Other Enigmas (London, 1978) 451. The notion of a speaker's 'implicit knowledge' of the language is, however, by no means unproblematic. See G. Evans, 'Semantic Theory and Tacit Knowledge' in S. H. Holtzmann and C. M. Leich, eds., Wittgenstein: to Follow a Rule (London, Henley, and Boston, 1981).
40. G. Frege, Posthumous Writings (Oxford, 1979) 197.
41. Ibid. 185.
42. See Bell, passim.
43. M. Dummett, Frege: Philosophy of Language (London, 1973) 305, 307.
44. P. F. Strawson, 'Meaning and Truth', in Logico-Linguistic Papers (London, 1971). See the critical discussion of this lecture in J. McDowell, 'Meaning, Communication, and Knowledge', in Z. van Straaten, ed., Philosophical Subjects (Oxford, 1980).
45. Habermas, Communication 1. See J. B. Thompson and D. Held, eds., Habermas: Critical Debates (London, 1982).
46. J. Habermas, Knowledge and Human Interest (London, 1972) 314.
47. Habermas, Communication 24. See also ibid. 24–5.
48. Ibid. 3.
49. Ibid. 146.
50. J. Habermas, Legitimation Crisis (London, 1976) 14. See also his 'Towards the Reconstruction of Historical Materialism', in Communication.

51. Habermas, *Communication* 1. See M. Rosen, 'Critical Theory: the Persistence of Philosophy', in S. Mitchell and M. Rosen, eds., *The Need for Interpretation* (London, forthcoming).
52. Habermas, *Communication* 177.
53. Habermas, *Knowledge* 328, n. 146.
54. D. Davidson, 'Radical Interpretation', *Dialectica*, vol. 27, no. 3–4 (1973), 315.
55. See Rosen, 'Critical Theory'.
56. W. V. O. Quine, *Word and Object* (Cambridge, Mass., 1970).
57. Davidson, 'Radical Interpretation' 324. See also 'Belief and the Basis of Meaning', *Synthese* 27 (1974), and 'Thought and Talk', in S. Guttenplan, ed., *Mind and Language* (Oxford, 1975). See C. McGinn, 'Charity, Interpretation, and Belief', *Journal of Philosophy*, 74 (1977), for a critique of the principle of charity, and R. Grandy, 'Reference, Meaning, and Belief', ibid., 70 (1973), for a modification of the principle adopted by G. Macdonald and P. Pettit, *Semantics and Social Science* (London, Henley, and Boston, 1981).
58. L. Wittgenstein, *Remarks on the Foundations of Mathematics* (Oxford, 1978) VI 39. This question is pursued in the contributions to Holtzmann and Leich, and in S. Kripke, 'Wittgenstein on Rules and Private Language', in I. Block, ed., *Perspectives on the Philosophy of Wittgenstein* (Oxford, 1981).
59. D. Davidson, 'The Method of Truth in Metaphysics', in P. A. French, T. E. Uehling, and H. E. Wettstein, eds., *Contemporary Perspectives in the Philosophy of Language* (Minneapolis, 1979) 295. Statements such as this, and that cited in the text to note 61 below make it difficult to accept Richard Rorty's claim that Davidson's project 'has no epistemological *parti pris*', *Philosophy and the Mirror of Nature* (Oxford, 1980) 257.
60. See D. Davidson, 'Truth and Meaning', *Synthese* 17 (1967), A. Tarski, *Logic, Mathematics, Metamathematics* (Oxford, 1969), and J. Wallace, 'On the Frame of Reference', in D. Davidson and G. Harman, eds., *The Semantics of Natural Language* (Dordrecht and Boston, 1972). M. Platts, *Ways of Meaning* (London, Henley, and Boston, 1979) expounds and defends Davidson's strategy.
61. Davidson, 'True to the Facts', *Journal of Philosophy*, 66 (1969) 758.
62. Davidson, 'Truth and Meaning' 311.
63. Davidson, 'Reality without Reference', in Platts, ed., *Reference* 139.
64. See M. Dummett, 'The Social Character of Meaning', in Dummett, *Truth*, 'What is a Theory of Meaning?' (I), in Guttenplan, and 'What is a Theory of Meaning?' (II), in G. Evans and J. McDowell, eds., *Truth and Meaning* (Oxford, 1976); see, in reply, C. McGinn, 'Truth and Use', and J. McDowell, 'On the Sense and Reference of a Proper Name', both in Platts, ed., *Reference*, J. Bouveresse, 'Frege, Wittgenstein, Dummett et la nouvelle "querelle du réalisme"', *Critique* XXXVI, no. 399–400, Aug.–Sept. 1980, and J. McDowell, 'Anti-Realism and the Epistemology of Understanding', in H. Parret and J. Bouveresse, eds., *Meaning and Understanding* (Berlin and New York, 1981).
65. Davidson, 'The Method of Truth' 298.
66. See C. McCabe, 'On Discourse', *Economy and Society*, vol. 8, no. 3, Aug. 1979.
67. See R. G. Collingwood, *An Essay on Metaphysics* (Oxford, 1940), and I. Lakatos, *Philosophical Papers* (2 vols., Cambridge, 1978).
68. H. Ishiguro, 'La Philosophie analytique et l'histoire de la philosophie', *Critique* XXXVI, no. 399–400, Aug.–Sept. 1980, 745. For a critical discussion of this attitude, see M. Ayers, 'Analytical Philosophy and the History of Philosophy', in J. Rée et al., *Philosophy and its Past* (Hassocks, 1978).
69. See A. J. P. Kenny, *Descartes* (New York, 1968) ch. 3.
70. J. L. Austin, *Philosophical Papers* (Oxford, 1970) 182.
71. P. F. Strawson, *Individuals* (London, 1959) 9, 10.
72. R. Rorty, editor's introduction, *The Linguistic Turn* (Chicago and London, 1967) 22.
73. D. Davidson, 'On the Very Idea of a Conceptual Scheme', *Proceedings and Addresses of the American Philosophical Association*, XLVII (1973–4).
74. G. A. Cohen, 'Freedom, Justice and Capitalism', *New Left Review*, no. 126, Mar.–Apr. 1981, 7.

75. See M. Foucault, *The Archaeology of Knowledge* (London, 1972), *L'Ordre du discours* (Paris, 1971), *Discipline and Punish* (London, 1977), and *The History of Sexuality*, vol. 1 (London, 1979).
76. McCabe, 280.
77. Gramsci, *Notebooks* 333.
78. See R. Johnson, 'Three Problematics', in J. Clarke *et al.*, *Working-Class Culture* (London, 1979).

Conclusion

1. L. Althusser, *Lenin and Philosophy and Other Essays* (London, 1971) 32–3. See also A. Callinicos, *Althusser's Marxism* (London, 1976) ch. 3.
2. Althusser, *Essays in Self-Criticism* (London, 1976) *passim.*
3. Althusser, *Lenin and Philosophy* 67.
4. I. Lakatos, *Philosophical Papers* (2 vols., Cambridge, 1978), ii ch. 13.
5. J. Habermas, *Knowledge and Human Interest* (London, 1972) 301–7.
6. Lakatos, *passim,* and K. R. Popper, *The Logic of Scientific Discovery* (London, 1968).
7. Althusser, *Philosophie et la philosophie spontanée des savants (1967)* (Paris, 1974).
8. G. W. F. Hegel, *Lectures in the History of Philosophy* (3 vols., London, 1963) iii. 428.
9. See R. Rorty, editor's introduction to *The Linguistic Turn* (London and Chicago, 1967).
10. K. R. Popper, *Conjectures and Refutations* (London, 1969) 72.
11. R. G. Collingwood, *An Essay on Metaphysics* (Oxford, 1940).
12. Althusser, *Lenin and Philosophy* 45.
13. See P. Anderson, 'The Antinomies of Antonio Gramsci', *New Left Review*, no. 100, Nov. 1976–Jan. 1977.
14. A. Gramsci, *Selections from the Political Writings 1921-1926* (London, 1978) 198.

Name Index

171

Name Index

Subject Index